FISHING BASICS

Gene Kugach

STACKPOLE BOOKS

Copyright © 1993 by Gene Kugach

Published by
STACKPOLE BOOKS
Cameron and Kelker Streets
P.O. Box 1831
Harrisburg, PA 17105

Printed in the United States of America

First Edition

10 9 8 7 6 5 4 3 2

Cover design by Gene Kugach

Library of Congress Cataloging-in-Publication Data

Kugach, Gene.
    Fishing basics : the complete, illustrated guide / Gene Kugach.
       p.   cm.
    ISBN 0-8117-3001-8
    1. Fishing.   I. Title.
    SH441.K84   1993
    799.1—dc20   92-28796
                                                                     CIP

CONTENTS

PREFACE

I am not a professional artist, a writer or an expert fisherman — I'm just an average guy who spent a lot of time gathering all the information presented in this book. I wrote it (drew it) because I feel a need for this type of a publication.

Although the information and drawings may have appeared in other forms, they have been modified or created for this book to best illustrate the points I want to make.

I tried to illustrate as much information as possible because, as they say, a picture is worth a thousand words.

Over the years I have read many articles and books and made sketches of what I feel are important facts relating to fish, fishing, lure making and fly tying. When I showed these sketches to my friends, they asked for copies and encouraged me to publish them.

The result is this book, *Fishing Basics,* which is what it really is, a bunch of notes and drawings relating to basic freshwater fishing that I would like to share with you.

Gene Kugach

To my wife, Bernadette
for all her support, encouragement, and patience

ACKNOWLEDGMENTS

It would be impossible to identify and credit all the sources on which I relied for the information in this book. Much of the factual data came from a variety of sources, including knowledgeable fishing individuals, fishing books, manufacturers' catalogs, monthly magazines, and so forth.

If I were to list each and every one of them, the list would become a book in itself; however, I would like to mention just a few that were extremely helpful.

Books and Pamphlets:
Fly Tying, John F. McKim
Complete Fly Tying Instruction Book, Hobby Bait Industries
Practical Flies and Their Construction, Gee and Sias
Publications by the Illinois Department of Conservation.

Magazines:
Midwest Outdoors, Outdoor Notebook, The In Fisherman, Fishing Facts, Sports Afield, Great Lakes Fisherman, Salmon/Trout/Steelheader, Fly Fisherman, Fly Rod and Reel, Fishing World, and Fins and Feathers.

Manufacturers' Catalogs:
Shakespeare, Eagle Claw, Mustad, South Bend, Orvis, Tackle-Craft, Trilene, Cortland, Grizzly Inc., Mister Twister, Northland Tackle Co., Lindy-Little Joe Inc., and Du Pont Stren.

In addition to all of the above, I would especially like to thank the members of the Chicago Fly Fishers Club, to whom I am indebted for the many hours of pleasure and the wealth of knowledge that they have shared with me.

Chapter 1

FISHERMAN'S ALPHABET

The ABCs of FISHING

The following pages contain illustrated key words in alphabetical order that relate to fishing.

I call them my "Fisherman's Alphabet." They cover some of the important basics you should know about fishing.

A. ATTRACTION

MAKE THE BAIT THE CENTER OF ATTRACTION.

To enhance the attractiveness of your bait, keep your equipment simple — use light gear, lines and hooks.

B. BAITING

WHEN BAITING UP, PUT THE BAIT ON PROPERLY.

Tie secure knots and hook the bait the right way.

C. CLEAN

KEEP YOUR HOOKS, LURES AND BAIT CLEAN.

Always remove weeds, algae, and the like from your hooks, lures, line, and bait.

Fisherman's Alphabet

D. DISTURB

DISTURB THE BOTTOM WITH YOUR BAIT OR LURE.

Give the bait or lure some action. Bounce it on the bottom.

E. EQUIPMENT

SELECT THE PROPER EQUIPMENT.

Use the right equipment for the type of fishing you will be doing: bait casting, spinning or fly fishing?

F. FIND

FIND THE BEST AREAS TO FISH.

Look for areas that provide cover for the fish.
Fish the bars, points, reefs and weed beds.
Try different places until you locate the productive areas.

G. GIVE

GIVE 'EM TIME TO TAKE THE BAIT.

Don't be too anxious to set the hook.
Let the fish run with the bait and give
them time to get the bait down.
Once you take it away, chances are
they won't pick it up a second time.

H. HOME

HOME IS WHERE
THE FISH LIVE.

Abrupt
change

"Home"
structure

I. IDENTIFY

BE ABLE TO IDENTIFY
YOUR CATCH.

Drop-offs, bars, points, reefs and
holes become "home" for fish. Fish
the edges where the bottom changes
abruptly.

Know your fish — learn to identify
them. Learn about their habits, the
food they like, their spawning season, and so on.

J. JUDGMENT

USE GOOD JUDGMENT WHEN SELECTING AREAS TO FISH.

Pick your spots according to the needs and habits of the fish. Learn to cast properly and accurately.

K. KNOTS

TIE YOUR KNOTS PROPERLY.

Learn the proper way to tie knots and take the time to tie your knots securely. Use plenty of working line. Pull your knot with a steady, even motion until it's tight. Don't trim the tag end too close.

L. LICENSE

ALWAYS CARRY A FISHING LICENSE.

Always buy a fishing license and carry it with you. It is illegal to fish without a license. Besides, most states use the license fees to improve fishing programs.

M. MAP

USE A CONTOUR MAP WHEN
POSSIBLE.

Try to get a map from the state or county, or from a bait shop near the lake you will be fishing.

N. NOISE

KEEP THE NOISE AT A
MINIMUM.

Don't scare the fish. Make as little noise as possible. Put your anchor in gently.

O. OBSERVE

OBSERVE OTHER FISHERMEN.

Ask questions of other people who are fishing. Ask what they caught, where they caught it, what bait they used, and so on.

Fisherman's Alphabet

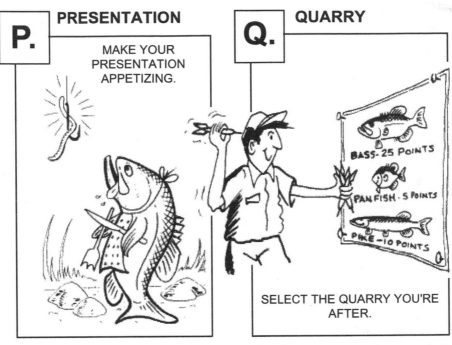

P. PRESENTATION

MAKE YOUR PRESENTATION APPETIZING.

Q. QUARRY

BASS - 25 POINTS

PAN FISH - 5 POINTS

PIKE - 10 POINTS

SELECT THE QUARRY YOU'RE AFTER.

Try different presentations: vary your retrieve, use different-colored lures, experiment with different baits.

Use the proper gear, lures, or bait for the type of fish you're after.

R. RIG

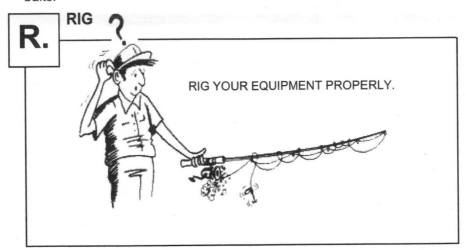

RIG YOUR EQUIPMENT PROPERLY.

Know your gear and how to rig it. Improperly rigged equipment will cause backlashes, tangles, and the possibility of losing a trophy fish.

S. STRUCTURE

ALWAYS FISH STRUCTURE.

Learn what it is and how it affects fish. Fish underwater points, drop-offs or bars, deep edges of weed beds, submerged logs, and so forth.

T. TEMPERATURE

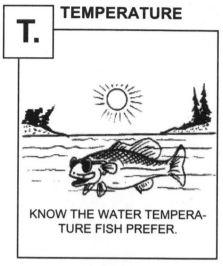

KNOW THE WATER TEMPERA-TURE FISH PREFER.

All fish species prefer certain water temperatures and seek out the depths that suit them best. Learn those depths and you'll catch more fish.

U. UTILIZE

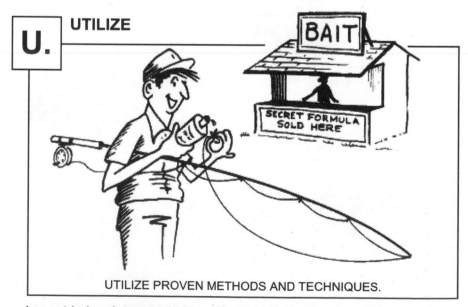

UTILIZE PROVEN METHODS AND TECHNIQUES.

Learn tried and true techniques like jigging, live lining, trolling, mooching, and still fishing. Find out what has worked for other anglers.

Fisherman's Alphabet

V. VARIETY

USE A VARIETY OF BAITS, LURES, AND OTHER APPROACHES.

If the fish aren't biting, vary your approach — your bait, your presentation, your rig — until you find what works.

W. WEATHER

WATCH THE WEATHER.

If you're on the water, keep an eye out for storms. Don't fish in a lightning storm. Watch the weather reports for approaching cold fronts and other threatening conditions.

X. "X" MARKS THE SPOT

MARK AN "X" ON YOUR MAP WHERE YOU'VE CAUGHT A FISH.

Keep records of your catches. Get a map of the lake you're fishing or make one and mark the spots that are productive.

Y. YIELD

USING "A" THROUGH "Z"
YIELDS RESULTS.

A THROUGH Z

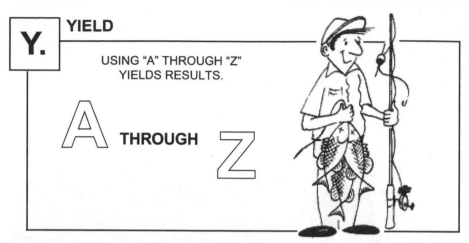

Learning the basics and applying them will result in successful fishing. Remember to make your bait the center of attraction, select the proper equipment, use good judgment and always fish structure.

Z. ZONE

FISH IN THE FISH ZONE — WHERE THE FISH LIVE

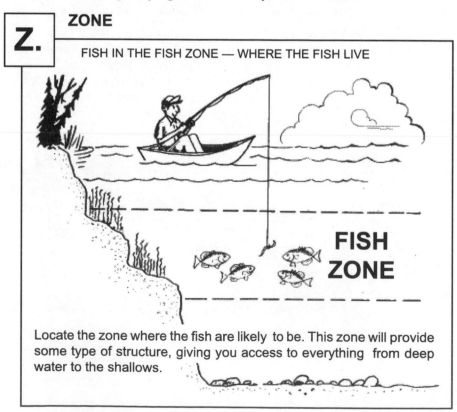

FISH ZONE

Locate the zone where the fish are likely to be. This zone will provide some type of structure, giving you access to everything from deep water to the shallows.

Chapter 2

HOW TO FISH

BAIT CASTING

Bait casting is one of the oldest methods used to catch fish. It gives you the ability to cast large lures (1/2 to 3/4 ounces) long distances.

The correct bait casting outfit consists of a rod with a good spring action, a good quality anti-backlash type reel (filled to capacity with a 10 –15 pound test line), and a variety of bait casting lures.

The following illustration shows the proper arm, wrist, and rod movements necessary to execute a good cast.

BAIT CASTING EQUIPMENT

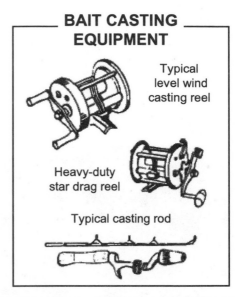

Typical level wind casting reel

Heavy-duty star drag reel

Typical casting rod

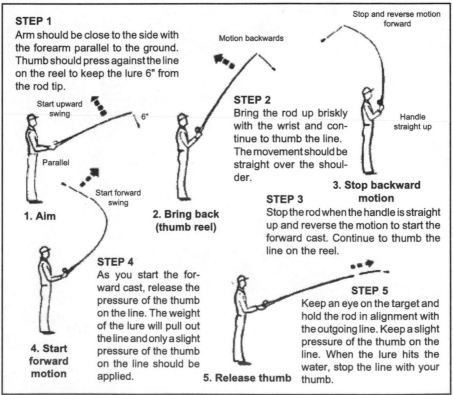

STEP 1
Arm should be close to the side with the forearm parallel to the ground. Thumb should press against the line on the reel to keep the lure 6" from the rod tip.

Start upward swing

6"

Parallel

Start forward swing

1. Aim

Motion backwards

STEP 2
Bring the rod up briskly with the wrist and continue to thumb the line. The movement should be straight over the shoulder.

2. Bring back (thumb reel)

Stop and reverse motion forward

Handle straight up

3. Stop backward motion

STEP 3
Stop the rod when the handle is straight up and reverse the motion to start the forward cast. Continue to thumb the line on the reel.

STEP 4
As you start the forward cast, release the pressure of the thumb on the line. The weight of the lure will pull out the line and only a slight pressure of the thumb on the line should be applied.

4. Start forward motion

5. Release thumb

STEP 5
Keep an eye on the target and hold the rod in alignment with the outgoing line. Keep a slight pressure of the thumb on the line. When the lure hits the water, stop the line with your thumb.

BAIT CASTING TIPS

The following illustrations show a few ways to improve your casting ability.

CASTING FORM

For better casting form, accuracy, and timing, keep the reel handle up when you execute a cast.

THUMB CONTROL

Reel handle should be up

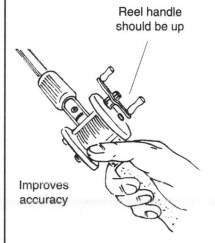

Improves accuracy

In addition to using your thumb to prevent backlash, use it as a brake against the spool when playing a running fish.

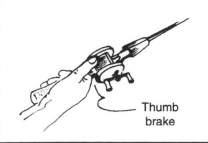

Thumb brake

ROD AND REEL NOMENCLATURE

The following illustrations identify the various parts of a bait casting outfit.

LEVEL WIND REEL

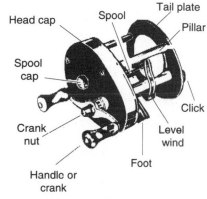

Head cap, Spool, Tail plate, Pillar, Spool cap, Click, Crank nut, Level wind, Foot, Handle or crank

STAR DRAG REEL

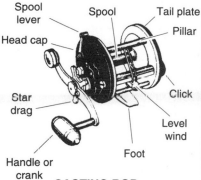

Spool lever, Spool, Tail plate, Head cap, Pillar, Star drag, Click, Level wind, Foot, Handle or crank

CASTING ROD OFFSET TYPE HANDLE

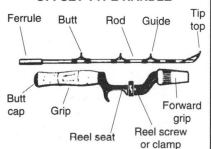

Ferrule, Butt, Rod, Guide, Tip top, Butt cap, Grip, Forward grip, Reel seat, Reel screw or clamp

SPIN CASTING

Spin casting has simplified fishing for everyone. It is virtually a foolproof means of casting light or heavy lures with no problems such as backlashes or line breakage.

The typical spin casting outfit consists of a 7-foot rod and a spinning reel (open face, closed face or spin cast) filled with monofilament line (between 6 and 10 pound test) that will allow casting lures that weigh 1/16 to 3/4 ounce.

The following illustrations show the basic steps necessary to execute a cast with a spinning outfit. The instructions are for an overhead cast using an open face reel.

SPINNING EQUIPMENT

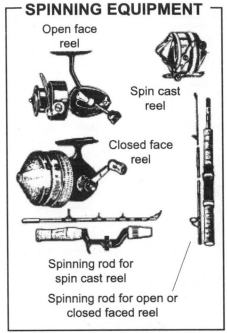

Open face reel

Spin cast reel

Closed face reel

Spinning rod for spin cast reel

Spinning rod for open or closed faced reel

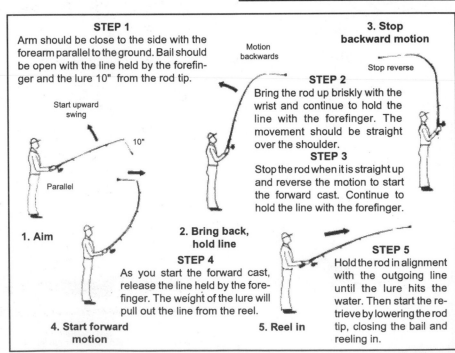

STEP 1
Arm should be close to the side with the forearm parallel to the ground. Bail should be open with the line held by the forefinger and the lure 10" from the rod tip.

Motion backwards

3. Stop backward motion

Stop reverse

Start upward swing

10"

Parallel

STEP 2
Bring the rod up briskly with the wrist and continue to hold the line with the forefinger. The movement should be straight over the shoulder.

STEP 3
Stop the rod when it is straight up and reverse the motion to start the forward cast. Continue to hold the line with the forefinger.

1. Aim

2. Bring back, hold line

STEP 4
As you start the forward cast, release the line held by the forefinger. The weight of the lure will pull out the line from the reel.

STEP 5
Hold the rod in alignment with the outgoing line until the lure hits the water. Then start the retrieve by lowering the rod tip, closing the bail and reeling in.

4. Start forward motion

5. Reel in

SPIN CASTING TIPS

Here are a few tips to try the next time you're out on the water.

LURE/FLY COMBO

Attach a fly on a leader behind or in front of your lure when the fishing gets tough. It will look like a minnow following the lure or a fish chasing a minnow.

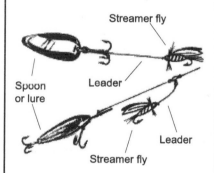

Streamer fly

Spoon or lure

Leader

Leader

Streamer fly

CASTING FLIES

You can cast some of those ultra-light flies by attaching a few split shot sinkers to the line about 12" forward of the fly.

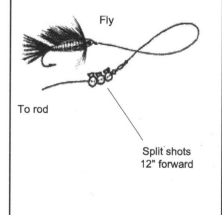

Fly

To rod

Split shots 12" forward

SPINNING GEAR NOMENCLATURE

The following illustrations identify the various parts of a spinning outfit.

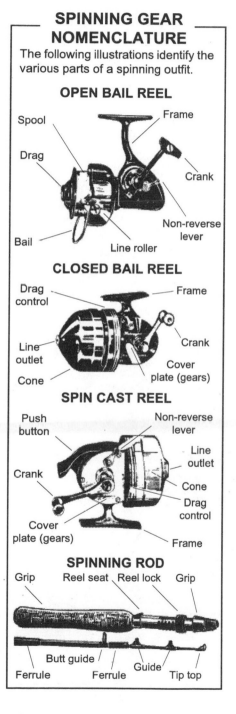

OPEN BAIL REEL

Spool

Frame

Drag

Crank

Bail

Non-reverse lever

Line roller

CLOSED BAIL REEL

Drag control

Frame

Line outlet

Crank

Cone

Cover plate (gears)

SPIN CAST REEL

Push button

Non-reverse lever

Line outlet

Crank

Cone

Drag control

Cover plate (gears)

Frame

SPINNING ROD

Grip

Reel seat

Reel lock

Grip

Butt guide

Guide

Ferrule

Ferrule

Tip top

FLY CASTING

Fly fishing is one of the oldest methods used to fish. It is still the best method for casting very light imitations of insects or other small lures and is considered by many to be the purest form of fishing.

The fly fishing outfit consists of an 8–9 foot long rod wlth either an automatic or a standard crank type reel, a balanced line, a tapered or monofilament leader, and an assortment of artificial flies or lures.

The following illustrations show the basic steps of fly casting.

FLY CASTING EQUIPMENT

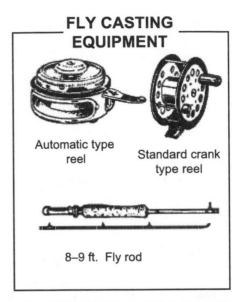

Automatic type reel

Standard crank type reel

8–9 ft. Fly rod

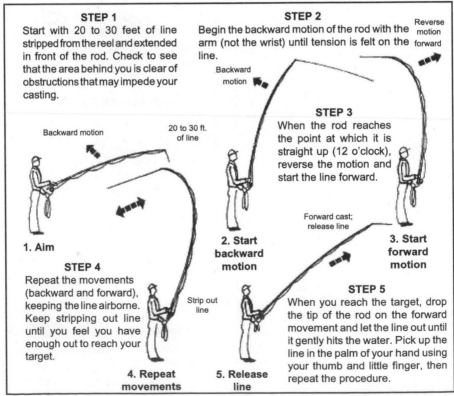

STEP 1
Start with 20 to 30 feet of line stripped from the reel and extended in front of the rod. Check to see that the area behind you is clear of obstructions that may impede your casting.

STEP 2
Begin the backward motion of the rod with the arm (not the wrist) until tension is felt on the line.

Backward motion

Reverse motion forward

STEP 3
When the rod reaches the point at which it is straight up (12 o'clock), reverse the motion and start the line forward.

Backward motion

20 to 30 ft. of line

Forward cast; release line

1. Aim

2. Start backward motion

3. Start forward motion

STEP 4
Repeat the movements (backward and forward), keeping the line airborne. Keep stripping out line until you feel you have enough out to reach your target.

Strip out line

STEP 5
When you reach the target, drop the tip of the rod on the forward movement and let the line out until it gently hits the water. Pick up the line in the palm of your hand using your thumb and little finger, then repeat the procedure.

4. Repeat movements

5. Release line

┌─ FLY CASTING TIPS ─┐

Here are a few tips to improve your fly fishing skills.

HAND RETRIEVE

This easy-to-learn hand retrieve is a must for every angler to know.

STEP 1
Grab line with thumb and first finger.

STEP 2
Hold with little and index finger.

STEP 3
Turn hand down and pick up next loop.

STEP 4
Fold in second loop with the first loop.

STEP 5
Repeat procedure, releasing each old loop before each grab.

STRIPPING

Rod hand

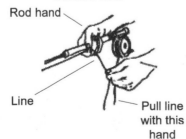

Line

Pull line with this hand

Hold line with thumb and forefinger of rod hand and pull back line with other hand.

┌─ NOMENCLATURE ─┐

AUTOMATIC REELS

Staff screw
Ratchet release ring
Ratchet coil case
Brake lever
Spool
Rod clip (foot)
Line protector
Spool
Ratchet coil case
Brake lever
Ratchet release ring
Staff screw
Rod clip (foot)

STANDARD CRANK TYPE REEL

Tail plate
Head cap
Spool
Handle
Spool cap and release
Pillar
Rod clip (foot)
Spool click

FLY ROD

Butt cap
Reel seat
Reel lock
Hand grip
Ferrule

Ferrule
Butt Section
Butt guide

Ferrule
Snake guide
Ferrule
Middle Joint Section

Ferrule
Snake guide
Tip top
Tip Section

FISHING LINES

Selecting the proper fishing line from the many that are available today can be a perplexing problem for anyone who fishes. However, there are a few points to consider when you make your selection.

Quality

Make it a point to purchase a quality line from a reputable manufacturer.

Proper Test

Select the line for the type of fishing you expect to do. Most sporting goods dealers will be glad to make recommendations if you ask them.

Proper Equipment

Purchase the proper line for the equipment you will be using. Spinning line won't work too well on a fly rod, so be sure you get the right kind of line for your equipment.

Remember

The most important thing between you and the fish is the line you use.

TYPES OF LINES

Bait Casting: Braided nylon, silk or dacron.

Spinning: Monofilament.

Fly Fishing: Braided nylon, silk or dacron impregnated in plastic.

ARBOR KNOT

The following knot is a simple, quick connection for attaching the line to the reel spool.

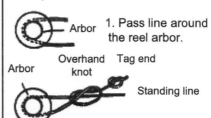

1. Pass line around the reel arbor.

2. Tie an overhand knot around the standing line and a second overhand knot in the tag end.

3. Pull tight and snip off the excess. Snug down first knot on reel arbor.

SPOOLING UP

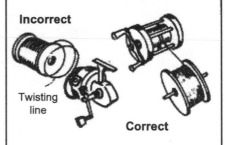

To avoid twisting, make sure the line comes off the spool onto the reel in the same direction. Fill the reel to within 1/8" of the spool lip as shown below.

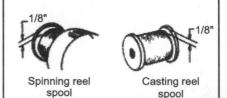

Spinning reel spool   Casting reel spool

FLY LINE SELECTION

The two major types of fly lines are the floating type and the sinking type. Each one is available in three de-signs: level, double tapered or weight forward. Consider the following infor-mation when you make your selec-tion.

FLOATING OR SINKING?

If you're fishing shallow water, use a floating type line. If you're fishing deep water, use a sinking type line.

WHICH DESIGN?

Line
Constant diameter

Level: Used when utmost distance is not required. Line has a constant diameter throughout the line length.

10 ft.
Tapered at each end

Double Tapered: Used for dry fly fishing to lay a fly delicately on the water. First 10 feet of line are tapered at both ends.

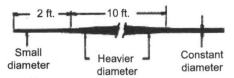
2 ft. — 10 ft.
Small diameter — Heavier diameter — Constant diameter

Weight Forward: Used for distance and casting bass bugs and bulky lures. Con-sists of a short section of small diameter line, followed by 8–10 feet of tapered heavier line.

── LINE CARE ──

The following illustrations show a few ways to avoid line damage.

FAULTY EQUIPMENT

Two of the major causes of line failure are faulty rod guides and burred reel surfaces. An easy way to check a rod guide is to use a cotton-tipped swab, as shown below.

Insert swab into guide
Cotton swabs

If swab becomes snagged, replace the guide.

REEL CHECK

Check bail
Check
line roller
Check spool

Make it a practice to periodically check your reel parts where your line makes contact. If you find any dam-age or wear, replace the part.

FRAYED LINE

Check your line for fraying by run-ning the line through your fingers.

HOOKS

Hooks come in an assortment of sizes and shapes. Some are used for specialized types of fishing or for a specific type of bait. The most important thing to remember when buying hooks is to look for hooks made by a reputable manufacturer. Cheap hooks lose fish.

PARTS OF A HOOK

The following illustrations show the various parts of a hook as well as the variations of the points, eyes, bend and the type of wire used in their manufacture.

VARIATIONS

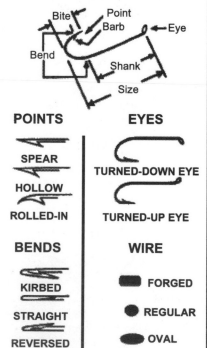

POINTS

SPEAR

HOLLOW

ROLLED-IN

EYES

TURNED-DOWN EYE

TURNED-UP EYE

BENDS

KIRBED

STRAIGHT

REVERSED

WIRE

FORGED

REGULAR

OVAL

TYPES OF HOOKS

SNELLED

COMMON

Short shank

Standard shank

Long shank

MISCELLANEOUS

Barbed

Weedless

Worm (plastic worm)

Salmon egg

Hump shank (poppers)

Double

Treble

Jig making

Pike

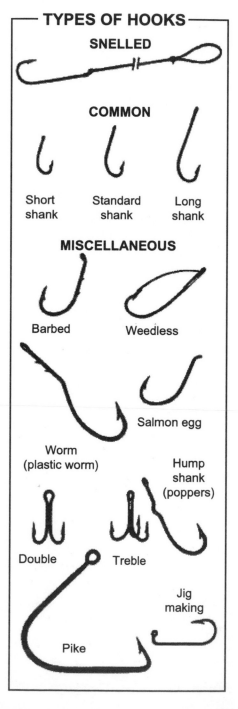

HOOK PATTERNS

There are hundreds of hook patterns, which differ according to their intended purpose. Some of the more popular patterns used in freshwater fishing are shown below.

COMMON PATTERNS

The pattern you use depends on the kind of fishing you plan to do and on your personal preference.

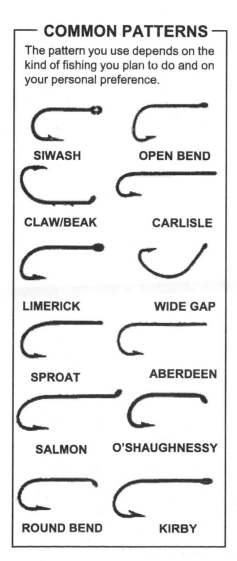

SIWASH   OPEN BEND

CLAW/BEAK   CARLISLE

LIMERICK   WIDE GAP

SPROAT   ABERDEEN

SALMON   O'SHAUGHNESSY

ROUND BEND   KIRBY

HOOK TIPS

Below are some tips for keeping your hooks sharp.

HOW TO POINT UP HOOKS

Start with the front edge.

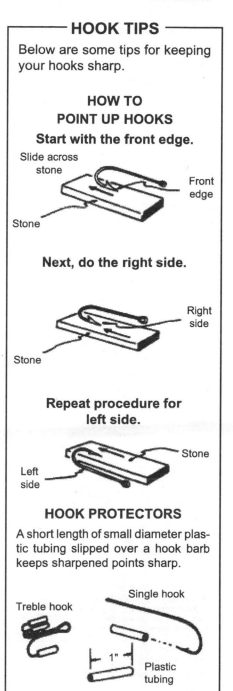

Slide across stone

Front edge

Stone

Next, do the right side.

Right side

Stone

Repeat procedure for left side.

Stone

Left side

HOOK PROTECTORS

A short length of small diameter plastic tubing slipped over a hook barb keeps sharpened points sharp.

Single hook

Treble hook

1"

Plastic tubing

BAIT HOOK SIZES: What Size Hook to Use

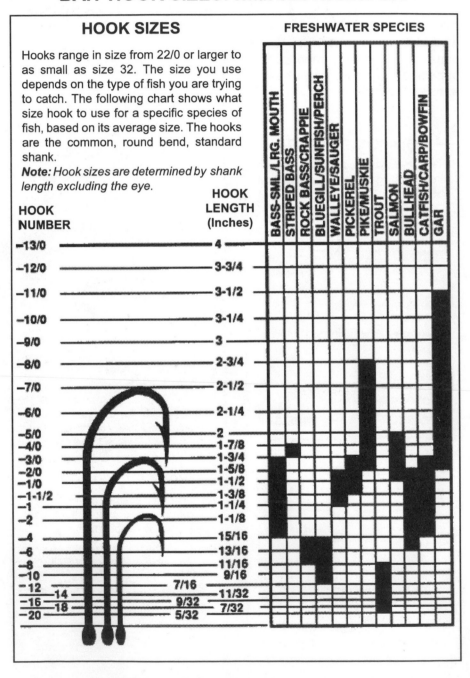

HOOK SIZES

Hooks range in size from 22/0 or larger to as small as size 32. The size you use depends on the type of fish you are trying to catch. The following chart shows what size hook to use for a specific species of fish, based on its average size. The hooks are the common, round bend, standard shank.

Note: *Hook sizes are determined by shank length excluding the eye.*

FRESHWATER SPECIES

HOOK NUMBER	HOOK LENGTH (Inches)
13/0	4
12/0	3-3/4
11/0	3-1/2
10/0	3-1/4
9/0	3
8/0	2-3/4
7/0	2-1/2
6/0	2-1/4
5/0	2
4/0	1-7/8
3/0	1-3/4
2/0	1-5/8
1/0	1-1/2
1-1/2	1-3/8
1	1-1/4
2	1-1/8
4	15/16
6	13/16
8	11/16
10	9/16
12	7/16
14	11/32
16	9/32
18	7/32
20	5/32

Species columns: BASS-SML./LRG. MOUTH, STRIPED BASS, ROCK BASS/CRAPPIE, BLUEGILL/SUNFISH/PERCH, WALLEYE/SAUGER, PICKEREL, PIKE/MUSKIE, TROUT, SALMON, BULLHEAD, CATFISH/CARP/BOWFIN, GAR

SNELL YOUR OWN HOOKS

The following illustrations show how to tie your own snelled hooks. One method uses an easy-to-learn simple knot, and the other method uses a fly-tying vise, bobbin, and thread.

SNELL KNOT

Insert one end of the leader through the hook eye and form a large loop. Pass the other end through the eye in the opposite direction.

Hold both lines along the shank and wrap the hanging line seven turns around both lines and the shank into tight coils.

Move fingers to hold coils in place and pull leader end until coils are snugged up neatly. Clip off tag end and tie loop knot in end of leader.

VISE VERSION

This type of snelled hook is made with a fly-tying vise in four simple steps.

STEP 1
Start with a piece of leader material and prepare it as shown below.

6 – 8 lb. test leader material

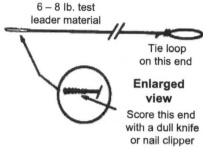

Tie loop on this end

Enlarged view
Score this end with a dull knife or nail clipper

STEP 2
Select your hook and clamp it into your tying vise. Wrap about 3/8" of the shank with waxed thread.

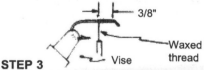

STEP 3
Slip the leader material through the hook eye and continue winding over the leader as tightly as possible. Tie off at the eye with three or four half-hitches.

Wind over leader, tie off with half-hitch

STEP 4
Paint the windings with brightly colored waterproof lacquer.

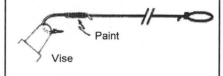

Paint

Vise

KNOTS

The following illustrations show how to tie some of the more commonly used fishing knots. Some helpful tips to remember when tying knots are:

1. Use plenty of working line.

2. Tighten knots with a steady, even motion.

3. Pull the knot tight.

4. Don't trim the tag end too close.

PERFECTION LOOP

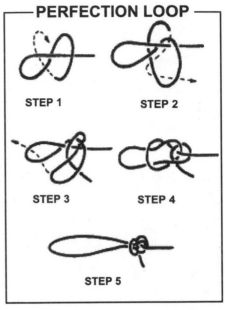

STEP 1   STEP 2

STEP 3   STEP 4

STEP 5

CLINCH KNOTS

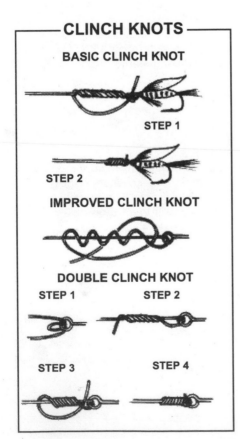

BASIC CLINCH KNOT

STEP 1

STEP 2

IMPROVED CLINCH KNOT

DOUBLE CLINCH KNOT

STEP 1   STEP 2

STEP 3   STEP 4

FISHERMAN'S BEND   FLY LINE LOOP

PALOMAR KNOT

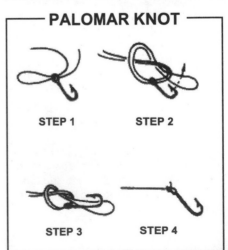

STEP 1   STEP 2

STEP 3   STEP 4

KNOTS

Knots are used for various purposes. The type of knot you use will depend on its intended application, such as attaching lures, hooks, sinkers, and so forth.

The following illustrations show a few additional knots to learn. By using them, you can improve your fishing ability.

KNOT SPLICE

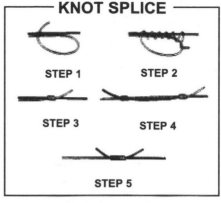

STEP 1 STEP 2

STEP 3 STEP 4

STEP 5

TURTLE KNOT

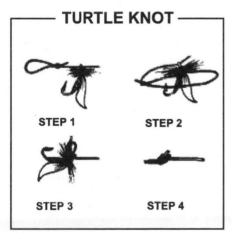

STEP 1 STEP 2

STEP 3 STEP 4

TWO-FOLD OPEN-EYE END

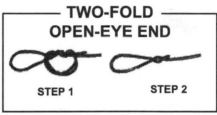

STEP 1 STEP 2

ALBRIGHT KNOT

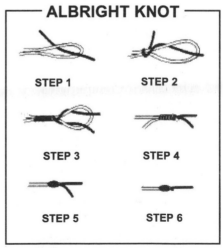

STEP 1 STEP 2

STEP 3 STEP 4

STEP 5 STEP 6

BLOOD KNOT

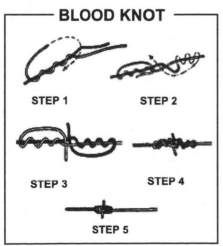

STEP 1 STEP 2

STEP 3 STEP 4

STEP 5

JOINER KNOT

EYE KNOT

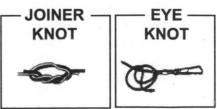

SINKERS

Sinkers come in various sizes and shapes and are used mainly to keep baits and lures at a desired depth in the water. They are basically made of lead and can be crimped or tied onto a fishing line. They also provide additional weight for casting or trolling. Sinkers are used in all types of fishing and should be just heavy enough to hold the bait where it's wanted.

A few examples follow of the proper uses for various types of sinkers.

BOTTOM FISHING

(1) Slip: Used for light biting fish, line slides through sinker.
(2) Dipsey: Used for surf or rocky bottoms, swivel keeps line from twisting.
(3) Lindy: Used for walleye rigs.
(4,5,6) Bank: Used for river or shore fishing, allows long distance casting.
(7) Snagless: Used in weeds or rocky bottoms.
(8,9) Pyramid: Used for sandy or mud bottoms, good holding power.

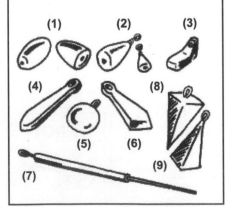

TROLLING

Trolling sinkers hold the bait or lure at a desired depth when trolling at a set speed.

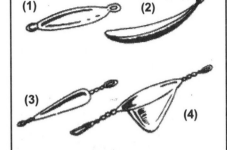

(1) Conventional: Line tied to one end, leader to the other.
(2) Snagless: For trolling in rocky or weedy areas.
(3) Torpedo: Used for added weight for lures when attached in front of the lure.
(4) Keel: For trolling in deep water, prevents the line from twisting.

STILL FISHING

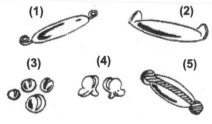

(1) Adjustable: Attached to the line by a coiled ring at each end.
(2) Clinch: Attaches to the line by crimping ears at each end to the line.
(3,4) Split shot: Crimps onto the line, ranges from BB size to large buckshot. Some types are removable and reusable.
(5) Rubber core: Attaches by twisting rubber core ears a half-twist in opposite directions after the line is inserted.

SINKER TIPS

The following illustrations show a few sinker applications to try the next time you're fishing, as well as a few tips on other sinker uses.

─ EXTRA WEIGHT ─

The next time you want to fish a fly or lure a little deeper, or have it sink a little faster, try the following.

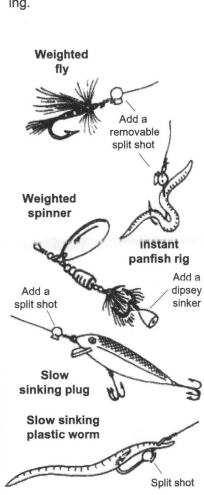

Weighted fly

Add a removable split shot

Weighted spinner

Instant panfish rig

Add a dipsey sinker

Add a split shot

Slow sinking plug

Slow sinking plastic worm

Split shot

OTHER APPLICATIONS

Besides sinking your bait, sinkers can be used for other applications as illustrated below.

─ FLY TYING ─

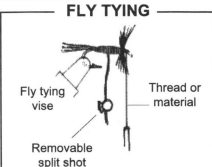

Fly tying vise

Thread or material

Removable split shot

When tying your own flies, a removable split shot attached to the loose end of your tying thread or material serves as extra hackle pliers.

MARKER BUOYS

A bank or pyramid sinker tied to a line and attached to an empty plastic bottle makes an excellent marker buoy to mark the hot spots to which you may want to return.

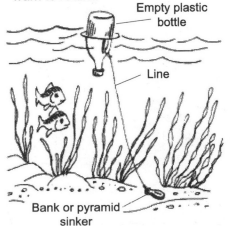

Empty plastic bottle

Line

Bank or pyramid sinker

SNAPS, SWIVELS, AND MORE

In addition to the hooks, lines, and sinkers, every tackle box should have an assortment of other items. The items shown below are only a few of the many that are available.

SNAPS

Snaps are a quick, convenient way to change hooks and lures. Below are examples of the different types that are available.

Basic   Basic with swivel

Safety   Safety with swivel

Safety wire   Ball bearing

Fly fishing

SWIVELS

Swivels are used to keep a lure or bait from twisting the line. They allow lures or bait to rotate without inhibiting their action.

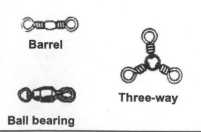

Barrel

Three-way

Ball bearing

WIRE LEADER

Wire leaders provide extra strength and toughness in front of the line to withstand the cutting teeth of larger fish.

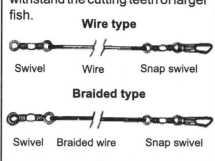

Wire type

Swivel   Wire   Snap swivel

Braided type

Swivel   Braided wire   Snap swivel

BAIT SPREADER

Bait spreaders are used to keep hooks apart or at the same level, or to hold hooks away from the line when using more than one.

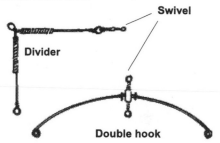

Swivel

Divider

Double hook

LEADER MATERIAL

Leader material is used for a multitude of fishing purposes (leaders, snelling, and so on) and is available in a variety of strengths and materials.

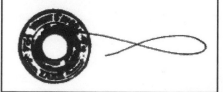

BOBBER FISHING

Bobbers are used as indicators to tell when a fish is biting. They are also used to keep the bait off the bottom or at a predetermined depth. They come in an assortment of sizes, shapes, and materials.

A few examples of the various types available today are shown below.

SLIP BOBBER SETUP

This is the most commonly used bobber setup for fishing at a predetermined depth. Here's how it works:

(1) A stop is placed on the line at a point that will stop the bobber at the desired depth to be fished.

(2) A bead and the bobber are added to the line and allowed to slide freely on the line.

(3) The hook is tied to the end of the line with a split shot sinker 12 inches above it.

The stop will pass through the rod eyes, allowing the bead and bobber to slide freely along the line to within 12 inches of the hook for easy casting. After the bobber is cast and hits the water, the weight of the bait and the split shot will pull the line down to the desired depth.

ASSORTED BOBBERS

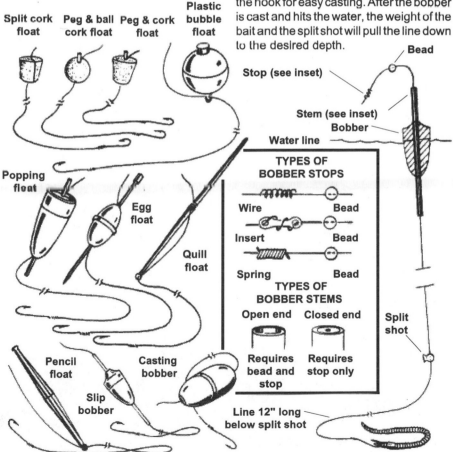

29

HOW TO
RIG LIVE BAIT

The following drawings illustrate how to attach live bait to a hook. These methods have proven to be very successful over the years.

MINNOWS

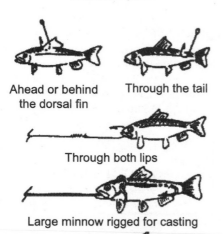

Ahead or behind the dorsal fin

Through the tail

Through both lips

Large minnow rigged for casting

Large minnow rigged with double hooks.

INSECTS

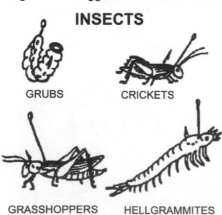

GRUBS

CRICKETS

GRASSHOPPERS

HELLGRAMMITES

WORMS

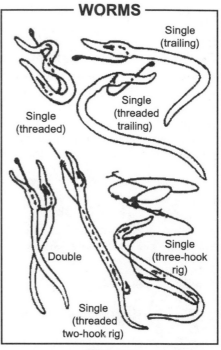

Single (trailing)

Single (threaded)

Single (threaded trailing)

Double

Single (three-hook rig)

Single (threaded two-hook rig)

FROGS

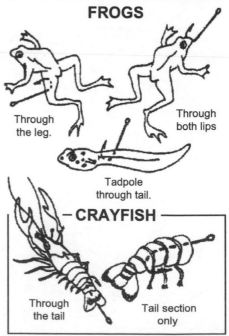

Through the leg.

Through both lips

Tadpole through tail.

CRAYFISH

Through the tail

Tail section only

RIGGING LEECHES, SUCKERS, AND WATERDOGS

In addition to baits such as minnows, worms, and so forth, leeches, suckers, and waterdogs can also be used as bait.

LEECHES

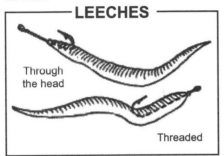

Through the head

Threaded

SUCKERS

Through the nose

WATERDOGS

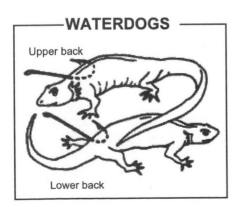

Upper back

Lower back

MINNOW SELECTION

The following illustration shows just a few of the more common minnows used as live bait.

CREEK CHUB
(Semotilus atromaculatus)
Used for: Northern pike and bass

GOLDEN SHINER
(Notemigonus crysoleucas)
Used for: Northern pike and bass

FATHEAD MINNOW
(Pimephales promelas)
Used for: Crappie, walleye, bass and panfish

BLUNTNOSE MINNOW
(Pimephales notatus)
Used for: Crappie, walleye and bass

BAIT FISH

The following illustration shows some of the wide variety of bait fish that can be used for fishing.

It is important to remember that bait fish kept in a container over a long period of time will die due to the lack of oxygen. To avoid this, you can add oxygen to the container by occasionally stirring the water or by changing it frequently. In addition, a number of products are available on today's market that can be used to add oxygen to the water, such as oxygen pills and battery operated pumps, which will extend the bait's life for longer periods of time. These products can usually be purchased at most bait shops or your local sporting goods store.

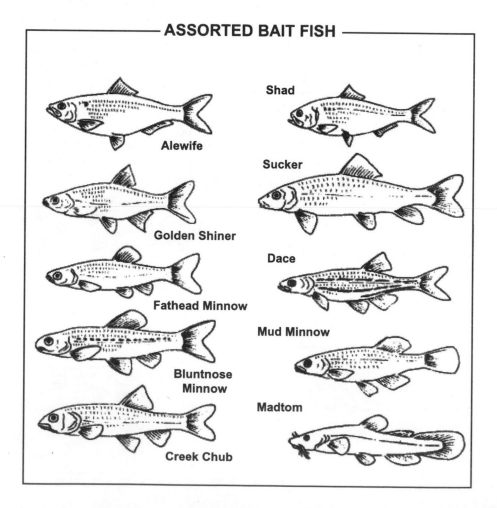

ASSORTED BAIT FISH

Alewife

Shad

Golden Shiner

Sucker

Fathead Minnow

Dace

Bluntnose Minnow

Mud Minnow

Creek Chub

Madtom

Chapter 3

FISHING TECHNIQUES

STILL FISHING

Still fishing can be done from an anchored boat, from a pier, from a bridge or from shore. You can use a hand line, a cane pole, or a rod and reel (bait casting or spinning), and any type of live or prepared baits. The bait is tossed out and left motionless in the water until a fish finds it and bites. Most types of fish can be taken by still fishing, but you will need a lot of patience to sit and wait for a fish to bite.

The bait can be fished on the bottom (no bobber) or off the bottom using a bobber or float. The size of the hooks and the bait that you use will depend on the species of fish you are trying to catch.

Still fishing can be done on ponds, lakes, rivers, and streams during most seasons and during any part of the day.

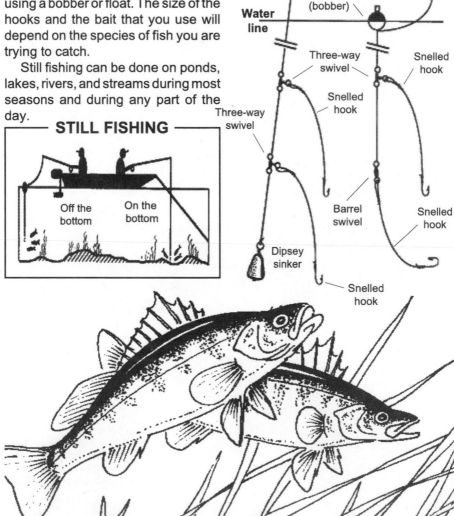

TYPICAL RIGS

BOTTOM RIG   OFF-THE-BOTTOM RIG

Float (bobber)

Water line

Three-way swivel

Snelled hook

Snelled hook

Three-way swivel

Barrel swivel

Snelled hook

Dipsey sinker

Snelled hook

STILL FISHING

Off the bottom   On the bottom

DRIFT FISHING

Drift fishing is done from a boat by trailing the fishing lines behind it as it drifts in the current or is pushed along by the wind.

Most any type of fishing equipment lends itself to drift fishing, whether it is a cane pole or a spinning outfit. Natural baits are the most productive, but jigs, lures, and artificial flies can also be used with good results.

The bait can be fished on the bottom (weighted) or at a desired depth by using a bobber or float. The size of the hooks and the bait will depend on the species of fish you are trying to catch.

Drift fishing can be done on ponds, lakes, rivers, and streams during any part of the day in most seasons.

The following illustration shows the types of rigs to use and how drift fishing works.

TYPICAL DRIFT FISHING RIGS

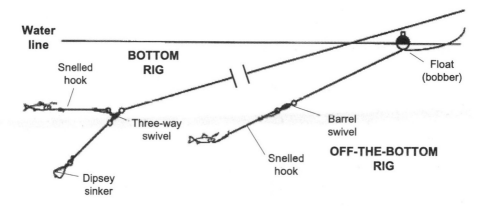

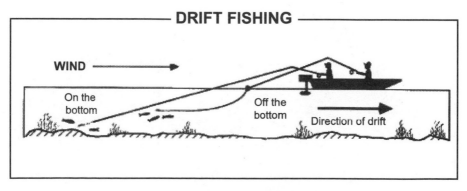

LIVE LINING

Live lining is generally done from an anchored boat when fishing a flowing body of water (streams or rivers). Any type of equipment can be used, such as a cane pole or spinning outfit, using live or prepared baits. The bait is usually fished on the bottom with the help of one or more small split shot sinkers to get it down, or in combination with a slip bobber, which raises the bait just off the bottom, allowing it to drift with the current over and through the holes and rocks where the fish may be holding.

The size of the hooks and the bait that you use will depend on the species of fish you are trying to catch.

Live lining can be done on rivers and streams during most seasons and any part of the day.

The following illustrations show how live lining works and the proper rigs to use.

TYPICAL LIVE LINING RIGS

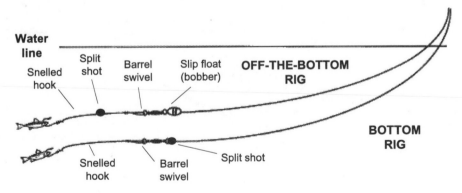

── LIVE LINING ──

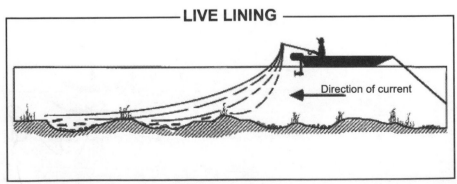

CHUMMING

Chumming is a method used to attract fish that involves throwing quantities of bait (chum) into the water where you are going to fish. The "chum" can be ground-up bait such as dead fish, cat or dog food, or cereals, or natural foods that can be stirred up from the bottom by using a stick, for example.

Chumming is an effective way of enticing fish into a feeding mood and overcoming their natural cautious nature.

Chumming can be done from shore or a boat, as shown in the following illustrations.

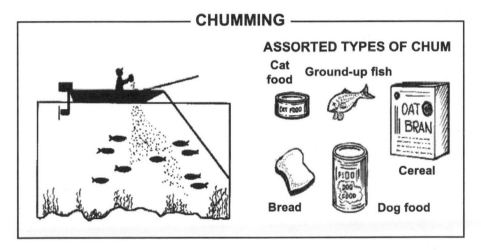

CHUMMING

ASSORTED TYPES OF CHUM

Cat food   Ground-up fish

OAT BRAN

Cereal

Bread   Dog food

BLUEGILL FISHING TIP

Try this tactic for catching bluegills the next time you're out fishing: Scatter a little cereal in the water before you start to fish and once they rise to feed, start fishing.

FLAKES

TROLLING

Trolling is generally done from a moving boat trailing artificial or natural bait behind it. You can also troll by towing a lure or bait while walking along the edge of a bridge, pier, or shoreline.

Any type of equipment can be used for trolling, from a cane pole to heavy big game fishing outfits, but spinning gear and bait casting equipment are the preferred choices.

The bait or lure is usually pulled behind the boat at a set speed, which governs the depth at which it will be fished. Trolling depth is determined by the species of fish you are trying to catch.

Trolling can be done during most any season and during any part of the day, but some states do not allow motors to be used when trolling. Check your local fishing laws regarding the use of a motor.

TYPICAL TROLLING RIGS

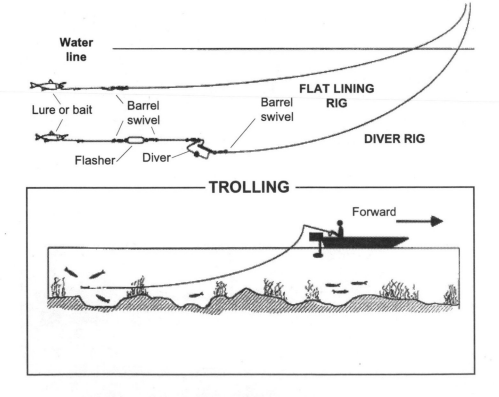

Water line

Lure or bait   Barrel swivel   Barrel swivel   **FLAT LINING RIG**

Flasher   Diver   **DIVER RIG**

TROLLING

Forward

MOOCHING

Mooching, a modified form of trolling from a boat, was developed for Pacific salmon fishing, and it can be used in large bodies of water such as the Great Lakes.

When mooching, a heavy sinker is used to take the bait deep. Then the boat is run forward a few yards, bringing the bait upward at an angle, before it is stopped or slowed until the bait returns to its original depth. The raising and lowering of the bait by moving the boat forward is a continuous process until a fish strikes.

The difference between standard trolling and mooching is the different depths that can be fished using the stop-and-go technique.

The same type of equipment that is used in trolling (spinning or bait casting gear) can be used when mooching, as well as natural or artificial baits.

TYPICAL MOOCHING RIG

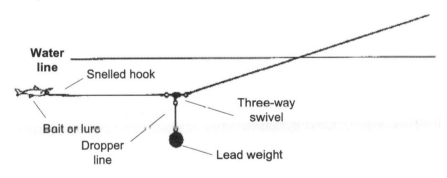

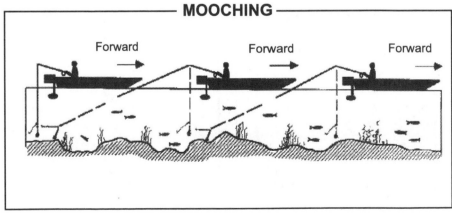

JIGGING

Jig fishing is rapidly becoming one of the most popular fishing methods used today. Unlike plug fishing, jigging requires the person who is fishing to create the action in the lure or bait that will attract the fish. This action is accomplished by moving the bait in an up-and-down or side-to-side motion.

To jig, you basically cast out and let the jig sink to the bottom, allowing a little slack in your line. Next, you take in the slack, drag the jig a few inches, and raise your rod tip with a quick jerk, bringing the jig up about a foot off the bottom. You then lower your rod tip, allowing the jig to hit the bottom, and continue repeating the up-and-down motion (side-to-side motion can also be inter-mixed) with the rod tip as you reel in.

Jig baits come in an assortment of sizes, shapes, and colors and can be used with or without live baits, depending on the jig type you are using. Jigging can be done from a boat or from the shore using either a spinning rig or a casting outfit. It can also be used when fishing deep waters where the fish are suspended. When fishing deep water for suspended fish, you lower the bait (jig) to the desired depth rather than allowing it to hit the bottom, and then create the necessary action by raising and lowering the rod tip with the quick jerks described above.

Jigging is an effective way to fish during any season or any part of the day. The following illustrations show how it works, along with some of the assorted types of jigs and rigs used today.

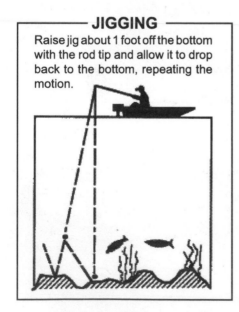

JIGGING

Raise jig about 1 foot off the bottom with the rod tip and allow it to drop back to the bottom, repeating the motion.

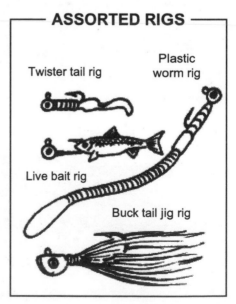

ASSORTED RIGS

Twister tail rig

Plastic worm rig

Live bait rig

Buck tail jig rig

JIG AND WORM FISHING

There are two basic methods used to fish with a jig and worm. The first is the "bottom hopping" or "bottom bouncing" method (Method "A"), in which you cast to the target, allow the jig to sink, and then start to reel in slowly, giving the rod tip a sharp twitch every third or fourth turn of the reel handle. The second method is the "swimming" or "sweep" technique (Method "B"), in which, after the cast, the jig is retrieved parallel to the bottom, with a taut line, as slowly as possible, keeping it moving in a steady and constant motion.

JIGGING METHODS

METHOD "A"

METHOD "B"

ASSORTED JIG SHAPES

Jigs come in an assortment of sizes and shapes. The following jigs are just a few examples of the wide assortment that is available.

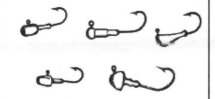

ASSORTED RIGS

A plastic worm can be rigged in many ways. Some methods use the standard jig, while others are rigged without any jig at all. The following rigs are just a few methods used in various parts of the country.

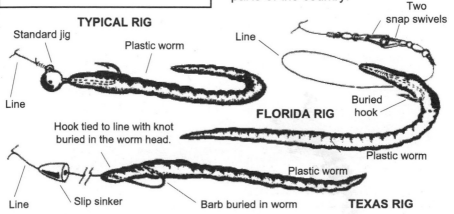

TYPICAL RIG

Standard jig

Plastic worm

Line

Line

Two snap swivels

Line

Buried hook

FLORIDA RIG

Plastic worm

Hook tied to line with knot buried in the worm head.

Line

Slip sinker

Barb buried in worm

Plastic worm

TEXAS RIG

BOTTOM BOUNCING

Bottom bouncing, a modified form of drift fishing or trolling, is an effective way to attract fish and cause them to strike or start feeding. Using buck tail jigs or natural baits, bottom bouncing is usually done from a moving boat (drifting or using a trolling motor) by dragging the bait or lure along the bottom, causing it to bounce along raising puffs of sand or mud. It is also an excellent method for locating fish when you are in unfamiliar waters. Once you get a few strikes while bottom bouncing, you can anchor up and apply other methods such as still fishing, jigging, or casting.

Remember when bottom bouncing to check your bait frequently for weeds and other debris that may be picked up as it moves along the bottom.

Bottom bouncing can be done during most seasons and during any part of the day. The following illustrations show a typical rig and how it works.

TYPICAL BOTTOM BOUNCING RIG

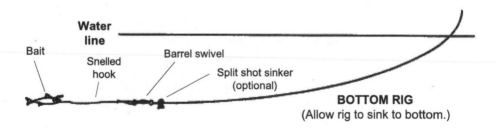

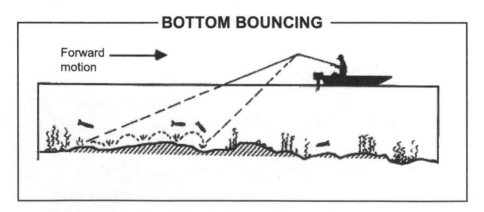

TROT LINE FISHING

Trot line fishing is a method especially suited for taking rough fish such as carp, bullheads and catfish. It is used frequently on rivers or streams that have a large population of rough fish.

Before you use this method of fishing, it would be wise to check your local and state regulations or any regulations governing the waters you will be fishing regarding trot lines. Trot line fishing is an effective method for taking great quantities of fish in a short period of time; consequently, many areas of the country restrict trot lines to prevent the over-harvesting of fish.

A trot line consists of a heavy line to which many baited hooks are attached at various depths. It is then strung between anchored floats or opposite banks of a river or stream and left unattended. An assortment of baits such as minnows, crayfish, stink, and prepared baits can be used to bait the line.

You can set a trot line during any part of the day, but usually you set it in the evening and leave it overnight until the following morning, at which time you check it to see what you've caught.

The following illustrations show the components of a trot line and how it is rigged.

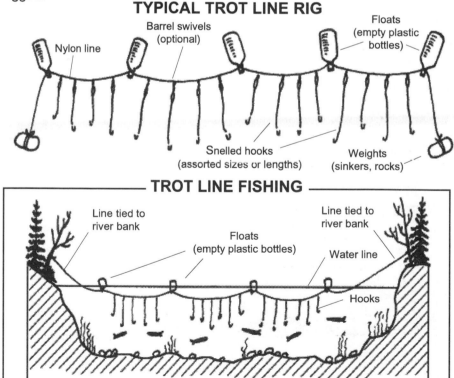

TYPICAL TROT LINE RIG

Barrel swivels (optional)

Nylon line

Floats (empty plastic bottles)

Snelled hooks (assorted sizes or lengths)

Weights (sinkers, rocks)

TROT LINE FISHING

Line tied to river bank

Line tied to river bank

Floats (empty plastic bottles)

Water line

Hooks

TROLLEY FISHING

Trolley fishing is a popular technique used for shore fishing in the Great Lakes region.

The rig consists of a heavy anchor tied to a chalk line, which is then thrown out into the water and allowed to sink. The chalk line is pulled slowly in until the anchor catches on the bottom, and then it is made as taut as possible and secured to a special pole anchored on shore. After the chalk line is set up, snelled hooks are attached to a special leader that has a trolley weight at one end and a retrieve line at the other end. The special trolley weight (pulley) is attached to the chalk line, on which it rides up and down. The hooks are then baited and lowered into the water by the trolley weight until they reach the desired depth to be fished.

The retrieve line is then slipped onto a bell device, which is attached to the special pole anchored on shore.

When a fish bites, the bell will ring, alerting the person who is fishing to set the hook. Once the hook is set, the fish is retrieved by pulling in the retrieve line. After removing the fish, the hooks are lowered back into the water.

The following illustrations show the components and how the trolley rig works.

HOW IT WORKS

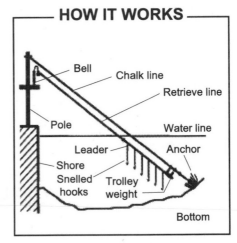

COMPONENTS

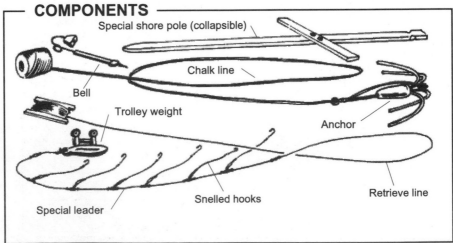

TROLLEY TIPS

The following tips can be useful when setting up a trolley rig.

ANCHOR TIP

In order to avoid losing your anchor if it gets wedged or hung up on the bottom, set it up as shown below.

Tie the chalk line to the anchor at the eye and just below the eye with a light test line or string.

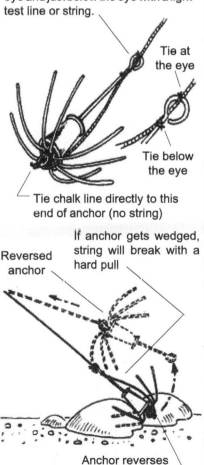

Tie at the eye

Tie below the eye

Tie chalk line directly to this end of anchor (no string)

Reversed anchor

If anchor gets wedged, string will break with a hard pull

Anchor reverses and pulls free

TOSSING THE ANCHOR

Two ways to throw out the anchor are the overhead toss and the underhand toss. The overhead toss allows for greater distance, but it can be difficult to control the direction of the anchor when it is released. With the underhand toss, the direction is a lot easier to control, but the distance of the toss will be shorter.

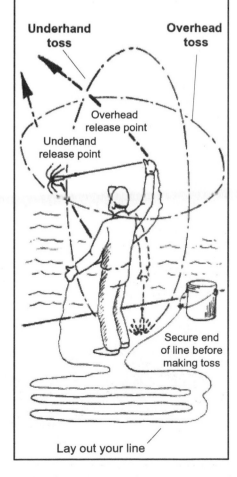

Underhand toss

Overhead toss

Overhead release point

Underhand release point

Secure end of line before making toss

Lay out your line

POWER LINE FISHING

Power line fishing is a technique developed by shore fishermen in the Great Lakes region. It consists of a 25–100 foot long rubber line with an anchor weight attached to one end and a special hook leader with a retrieve line attached to the opposite end.

The weighted end is tossed out as far as possible and allowed to sink and anchor to the bottom. Once the weight is anchored, the retrieve line is pulled in by stretching the rubber line until the special leader is exposed. Snelled hooks are then added to the leader and baited, and the line is returned into the water by releasing the tension on the rubber line.

The retrieve line is then attached to a bell device on shore, which signals that you've gotten a bite, allowing you to set the hook.

After the hook is set, the fish is pulled in by the stretching effect of the rubber line.

The illustrations below show how a power line works and all of the components.

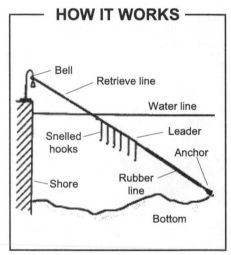

HOW IT WORKS

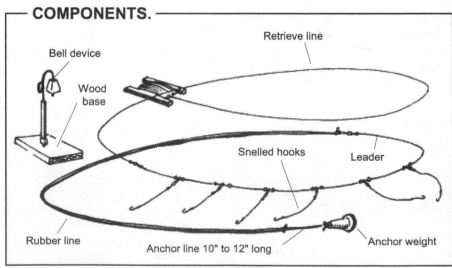

COMPONENTS.

POWER LINE TIPS

The following are just a few tips that can be useful when setting up a power line rig.

ANCHOR TOSS

To get greater distance when you toss out the anchor weight, rig the weight as shown below. The extra chalk line allows the weight to be swung overhead or underhand rather than just being thrown.

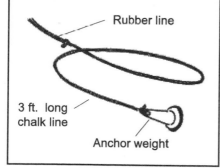

Rubber line

3 ft. long chalk line

Anchor weight

BELL SETUP

A 4" long 2" x 4" piece of wood makes a great base for a bell alarm and takes up very little space in the tackle box.

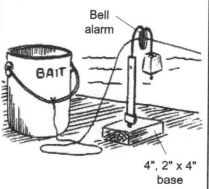

Bell alarm

BAIT

4", 2" x 4" base

MAKE YOUR OWN HOOK LEADER

MATERIALS REQUIRED

8 ft. long, 10 lb. test mono line
6 snap swivels
2 barrel swivels
12 red beads
12 connector sleeves

STEP 1

Tie one of the barrel swivels onto the end of the mono line.

Line Barrel swivel

STEP 2

Slip a connector sleeve, a bead, and a snap swivel onto the line. Tie an overhand knot on the snap swivel 12" away from the barrel swivel and slip on a second bead and connector sleeve. Repeat this step every 12" with all the snap swivels.

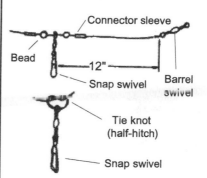

Connector sleeve

Bead

12"

Snap swivel

Barrel swivel

Tie knot (half-hitch)

Snap swivel

STEP 3

After all the snap swivels are tied in place, snug up the beads and the connector sleeves to each side of the snap swivels and gently crimp the sleeves with a pair of pliers.

Connector sleeve

Bead

Knot

Snap swivel

STEP 4

Repeat step 1 at the opposite end of the line 12" from the last barrel swivel.

SMELT FISHING

Every year from April to May, people who fish the Great Lakes gather along the lake shores in pursuit of the "American smelt." Each spring this small fish ascends rivers, streams, and shallow beaches shortly after nightfall to spawn. To catch these tasty little fish, fishermen set up their special rigs just before sunset and fish throughout the night until daybreak.

The most commonly used smelt fishing rig consists of a chalk line, a trolley weight, an anchor, a gill net, a retrieve line, and a lantern.

To set the rig up, the anchor which is attached to the chalk line is tossed out, and the line is pulled in until the anchor takes hold of the bottom. The chalk line is made as taut as possible and the line is then tied to a pole. After the line is secured to the pole, a gill net with a trolley weight and a retrieve line is attached to the chalk line.

The gill net is then lowered into the water by the trolley weight, which rides up and down on the chalk line on wheels, allowing the net to be lowered or raised with the retrieve line.

The net is left in the water for an average of ten minutes and then it is checked to see what was caught by raising it to the surface.

The following illustrations show the basic components of a smelt rig and how it works.

HOW IT WORKS

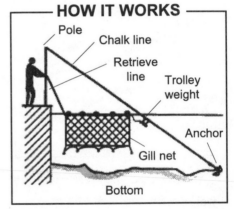

COMPONENTS

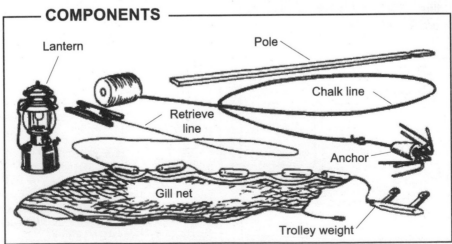

SMELTING TIPS

The following illustrations give just a few tips to remember relating to smelt fishing.

NET REPAIRS

It's a good idea to stretch out a net and examine it for holes or snags. Most simple repairs can be made by "granny-knotting" as shown below.

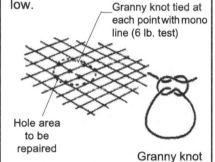

Granny knot tied at each point with mono line (6 lb. test)

Hole area to be repaired

Granny knot

NET CHECKS

In addition to checking for holes and snags, check the floats and weights on the top and bottom lines of your net to insure that they are secure.

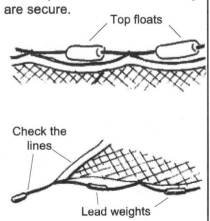

Top floats

Check the lines

Lead weights

TROLLEY CARE

It's a good practice to oil the wheels of the trolley weight each time you use it. A little silicone spray will keep the wheels in good working order.

Apply spray to the trolley wheels.

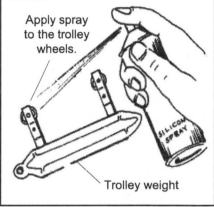

Trolley weight

SMELT FACTS

American Smelt
(Osmerus mordax)

Smelt grow to a length of 14 inches, but the average spawning fish is only 7 to 8 inches in length.

■ ■ ■

Smelt usually begin their spawning runs in mid-March or early April. When the water temperature reaches 38 degrees, it is warm enough to trigger their inshore migration.

■ ■ ■

Smelt are coastal natives from the Gulf of St. Lawrence to the Chesapeake Bay. They are landlocked in many New England lakes and all of the Great Lakes, where they were introduced by the building of the St. Lawrence seaway.

MARKING LOCATIONS

When you are out fishing on a lake or river and you hit a hot spot that you would like to locate and fish another time, try the methods shown below to find and mark the location for another day.

── "V" SIGHTING METHOD (TWO-POINT SIGHTING) ──

Always start by "sighting" two objects on either shore. Select objects that are permanent, such as buildings, trees, and poles. If possible, keep your sight lines in a "V" shape for the most accurate reading. Sight lines at 45-degree angles will also work; beyond that, the accuracy drops off. If you have a map of the lake or river, record your sightings for future reference.

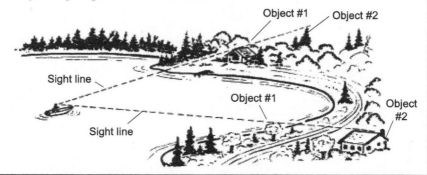

── "T" SIGHTING METHOD (THREE-POINT SIGHTING) ──

With this method, you need an object such as a boat oar or your fishing pole along which to sight. Place the oar or fishing pole across the boat (perpendicular to the bow) and sight along it to your left and right sides, picking landmarks on the shore. Always select objects that are permanent, such as buildings, trees, and poles. Next, sight forward along the boat bow to select the third point. If you have a map of the lake or river, record your sightings for future reference.

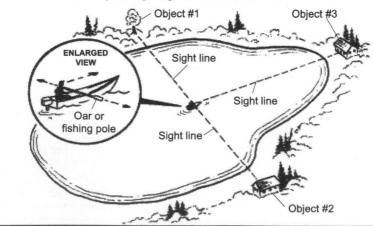

Chapter 4

ICE FISHING

ICE FISHING BASICS

The most important consideration to make when ice fishing is what to wear. With the proper warm clothing and a good pair of boots, ice fishing can be an enjoyable sport, but if you're improperly dressed, it can be a miserable experience.

Today, you can choose from a variety of garments designed specifically for winter conditions. Thermal underclothing, outer garments, insulated boots, and rubberized gloves are all available for ice fishing at a reasonable cost. All of these items are a must if you plan to pursue the sport. You should also include a pair of sunglasses as part of your outfit to reduce the glare from the ice when you are fishing.

Once you've made your clothing selection, the next step is to select your equipment. Most ice fishing equipment can be purchased inexpensively, but quite a bit of it can be homemade as shown on the following pages.

The following illustrations show some of the basic equipment you will require.

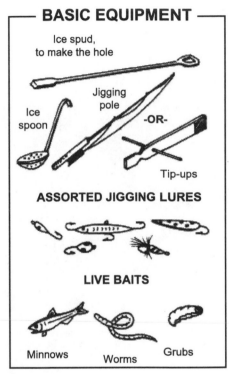

BASIC EQUIPMENT

Ice spud, to make the hole

Ice spoon

Jigging pole

-OR-

Tip-ups

ASSORTED JIGGING LURES

LIVE BAITS

Minnows   Worms   Grubs

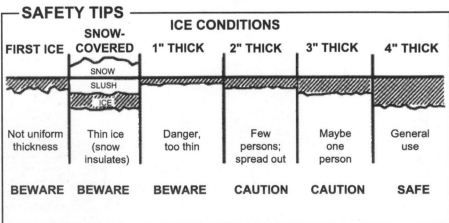

SAFETY TIPS

ICE CONDITIONS

FIRST ICE	SNOW-COVERED	1" THICK	2" THICK	3" THICK	4" THICK
	SNOW				
	SLUSH				
	ICE				
Not uniform thickness	Thin ice (snow insulates)	Danger, too thin	Few persons; spread out	Maybe one person	General use
BEWARE	BEWARE	BEWARE	CAUTION	CAUTION	SAFE

ICE FISHING TIPS

Try the following time-proven tips the next time you're on the ice.

HOLE COVER

A piece of 1-ft. square carpet or floor tile prevents ice hole freeze-up and keeps out drifting snow. All you need to do is cut out a slot for your line as shown below.

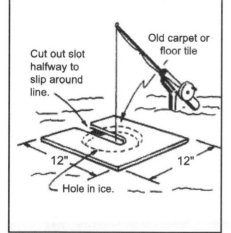

Cut out slot halfway to slip around line.

Old carpet or floor tile

12" 12"

Hole in ice.

DEPTH MARKER

Thread line through shirt button and adjust to desired depth.

A small shirt button makes an excellent adjustable marker when you want to keep your bait at the right depth.

HOMEMADE GAFF

It's a good practice to take along a gaff when ice fishing. You never know when a lunker pike or bass will take your bait and you will need a gaff to pull him out. The following illustration shows how to make your own gaff, which is as good as a store-bought gaff.

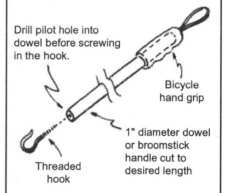

Drill pilot hole into dowel before screwing in the hook.

Bicycle hand grip

1" diameter dowel or broomstick handle cut to desired length

Threaded hook

After the hook is in place, sharpen the point with a file.

5-GALLON CARRYALL

An empty 5-gallon plastic bucket can be used to carry gear and the fish you catch. It's also something to sit on when ice fishing.

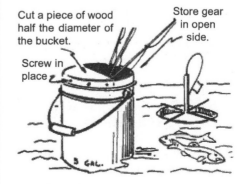

Cut a piece of wood half the diameter of the bucket.

Store gear in open side.

Screw in place

5 GAL.

ICE FISHING TIPS

The following tips will be useful for ice fishing.

RUBBER BAND BOBBERS

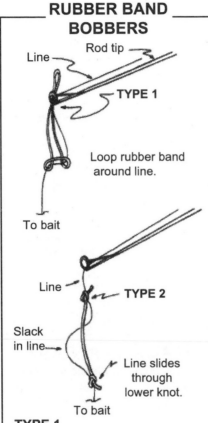

Line

Rod tip

TYPE 1

Loop rubber band around line.

To bait

Line

TYPE 2

Slack in line

Line slides through lower knot.

To bait

TYPE 1
Rubber band is looped around the line and slipped through the rod eye. When a fish bites, the rubber band slips out.

TYPE 2
Rubber band is tied to the line at both ends with slack line between the knots. When a fish bites, it stretches and the line slides through the lower knot.

BAIT RIGS

The following examples are just a few ways to rig your bait.

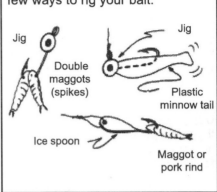

Jig

Jig

Double maggots (spikes)

Plastic minnow tail

Ice spoon

Maggot or pork rind

EMERGENCY BAITS

Try the following if you run out of bait or if the fishing slows down.

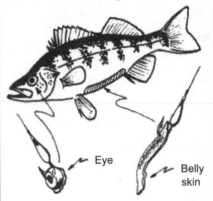

Eye

Belly skin

Use the eyes from the fish you already caught. Eyes make exceptional bait, and it is seldom necessary to rebait the hook more than once or twice in the course of a day's fishing. You can also try a piece of belly skin about 1/2 inch long and 1/8 inch wide, hooked at one end.

MAKE YOUR OWN ICE FISHING RODS

If you happen to break a fly rod or a spinning rod, don't throw it away. With a little effort, you can make yourself a couple of ice fishing chugging rods with the pieces.

STEP 1

Using a hacksaw, trim the handle part of the rod at the last eye, as shown in the drawing below. This will make a great rod for larger fish.

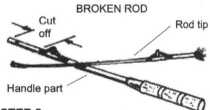

BROKEN ROD

Cut off

Rod tip

Handle part

STEP 2

Cut the remaining broken tip, as shown below, and by following the simple instructions in steps 3 through 6, you can make yourself a second rod for panfish.

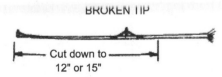

BROKEN TIP

Cut down to 12" or 15"

STEP 3

Handle: Using a 12" long piece of broomstick or a 1" diameter dowel rod, drill a hole 2" deep into one end with a diameter large enough to insert the base of the rod tip.

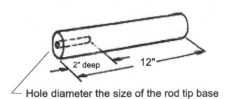

2" deep   12"

Hole diameter the size of the rod tip base

STEP 4

Using epoxy cement, glue the rod tip into the handle.

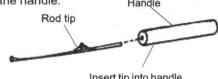

Handle

Rod tip

Insert tip into handle and glue into place.

STEP 5

Wire line holder: Take a 6" long piece of wire and form it as shown below with a pair of pliers.

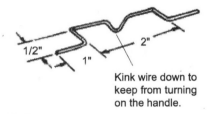

1/2"   1"   2"

Kink wire down to keep from turning on the handle.

STEP 6

After the wire line holder is formed, tape it to the handle as shown below.

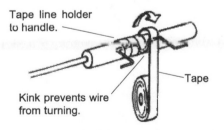

Tape line holder to handle.

Kink prevents wire from turning.

Tape

Note: The wire line holder can be added to the handle part of the rod, or you can use your reel for larger fish.

FINISHED CHUGGING ROD

ATTRACTORS

Attractors are used to bring fish into a given fishing area or, when used along with a lure, to direct them to the bait.

—ATTRACTOR RIG —

The following rig, using a Dardevle Spoon with the hook removed as an attractor, has produced excellent results.

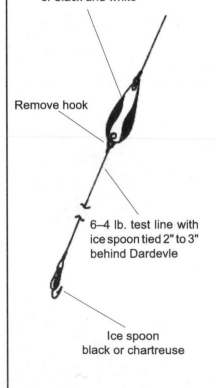

1/32 oz. Eppinger Dardevle (Skeeter model) copper or black and white

Remove hook

6–4 lb. test line with ice spoon tied 2" to 3" behind Dardevle

Ice spoon
black or chartreuse

HOMEMADE ATTRACTOR

HOOKLESS BLUEGILL ATTRACTOR

Barrel swivel

Connector sleeve

Drill hole, trim off corners

Aluminum soda or beer can tab

— ASSEMBLY —

STEP 1
Attach sinker with connector sleeve to a 24" long piece of wire or mono leader material.

STEP 2
Crimp on connector sleeve 3" from sinker.

STEP 3
Slip on bead.

STEP 4
Slip on can tab blade.

STEP 5
Slip on second bead.

STEP 6
Crimp on the second connector sleeve 3" from the last connector.

STEP 7
Repeat steps 3,4,5,6 for each blade to be added up to the swivel.

Dipsey sinker

HOW IT WORKS

Drop the attractor through the hole in the ice down to the fish zone. Jig it up and down to get the blades flashing, then pull out the attractor and drop down your baited line.

PANFISH KILLER

Here's a simple little lure you can make that is truly a panfish killer. It is so simple that you can make it in a couple of minutes and the results will be worth the effort when it's properly fished.

INSTRUCTIONS

All you need to make yourself some of these dandy lures is some prism paper (adhesive backed) and some #10 hooks.

STEP 1

Cut out 1/4" diameter circles from the prism paper (any color).

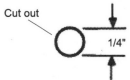

Cut out — 1/4"

Be sure diameter of prism paper is as close to 1/4 " as you can get it when cut.

STEP 2

Remove the backing and fold it in half around the shank of the hook, as shown below.

Fold

Your lure is now complete and ready to use.

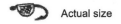

Actual size

HOW TO USE IT

The key to making the panfish killer perform properly in the water is the way you rig it. The following illustration shows the proper rigging.

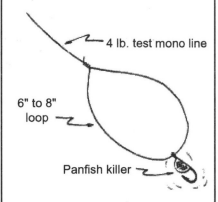

4 lb. test mono line

6" to 8" loop

Panfish killer

Important: Don't forget the loop. It's the loop in the line that makes the lure flutter on its way down, which tantalizes the fish. Without the loop, NO FLUTTER!

LIVE BAIT COMBINATION

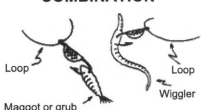

Loop

Loop

Wiggler

Maggot or grub

The panfish killer works best when used in combination with live bait. Hook on a grub, wax worm, maggot, or a wiggler for the best results.

MAKE YOUR OWN ICE SPOONS

You can make your own ice spoons easily with a few basic tools that can be found in the average home. Even if you don't ice fish, ice spoons are great to use all year long. They can be fished with a fly rod or a spinning outfit, and the results can be fantastic.

Below are a few examples of the different shapes you can make using the instructions on the following page.

ASSORTED SPOONS

EQUIPMENT

SOLDERING IRON

SPINNER BLADES

HOOKS
#10–#12

Colorado Willow Indiana
Sizes: 00, 0, or 1

BEADS

Nickel Copper Red
Sizes: #5 and #6

SOLDER

LONGNOSE PLIERS

EPOXY CEMENT

MAKE YOUR OWN ICE SPOONS

┌─ BEAD TYPE SPOONS ─┐

The beaded type spoons are the easiest to assemble.

All you need is some epoxy cement, some beads, hooks and a styrofoam block to hold them as they dry.

STEP 1.

Slip the bead over the hook eye. Use a No. 5 bead with the size 12 hook and a No. 6 bead for the size 10 hook.

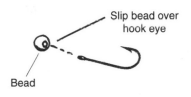

Slip bead over hook eye

Bead

STEP 2.

Dab a drop of epoxy cement over both ends of the hook shank where the bead rests.

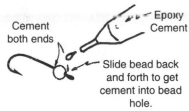

Cement both ends

Epoxy Cement

Slide bead back and forth to get cement into bead hole.

Step 3.

After the bead is cemented, stick the hook barb into the styrofoam block and let it dry.

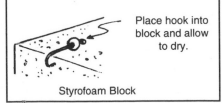

Place hook into block and allow to dry.

Styrofoam Block

┌─ BLADE TYPE SPOON ─┐

The blade type spoon requires a little more effort to make than the bead type, however it is not that difficult to assemble.

STEP 1.

Clean the surface of both the hook and the blade that are to be soldered together.

Use a fine sandpaper or emery cloth for cleaning.

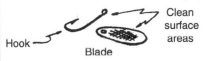

Hook

Blade

Clean surface areas

STEP 2.

Secure the blade to a piece of wood (wood block) using a small tack or nail. This allows both hands to be free for the next step.

Wood Block

Tack or Nail

Blade

STEP 3.

Next select the proper hook and hold the hook in position using the longnose pliers over the blade as shown below. Solder the hook to the blade, adding additional solder until it is firmly in place.

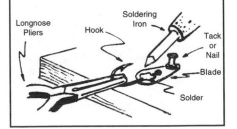

Longnose Pliers

Hook

Soldering Iron

Tack or Nail

Blade

Solder

MORE TIPS

The following are some additional tips on ice fishing which can be beneficial the next time your out on the ice.

PICKING THE RIGHT SPOT

Unless your familar with the water you are planning to fish or you have a depth sounder, picking the right spot to make your hole(s) in the ice can present a problem. Here's a trick to try when your fishing some of those smaller lakes or ponds.

Get down on your knees and look through the ice to see what type of bottom structure will be below you. In most cases, if the lake or pond is free of snow cover, you will be able to see the bottom. Look for some form of structure or cover (weed-beds, dropoffs, rocks, or sunken logs) before making your hole.

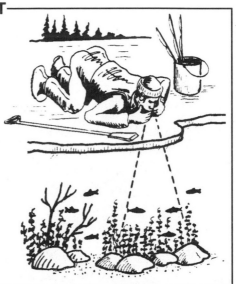

CHAFING LINES

Chafing your line on the edge of the hole is unavoidable, but you can reduce the frequency by trying the following tip. After you drill or cut your hole, use an ice pick to smooth off the edges, especially the ones beneath the ice.

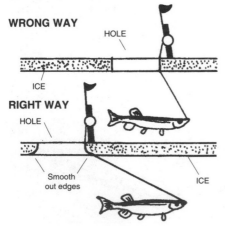

WRONG WAY

HOLE

ICE

RIGHT WAY

HOLE

Smooth out edges

ICE

WARM FEET

Here's a way to keep your feet from getting cold while sitting on the ice. The next time you're out, take along a board that is large enough to place your feet on. The wooden board will keep your feet off the ice, and they will stay warmer for a longer period of time.

Chapter 5

FISHING RIGS

BASIC RIGS

The following illustrations show various ways to rig flies, spoons, plugs and jigs for trolling, casting, fly fishing, and spinning.

CASTING RIGS

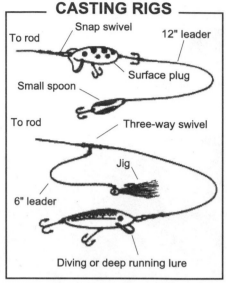

Snap swivel
To rod
12" leader
Surface plug
Small spoon

To rod
Three-way swivel
Jig
6" leader
Diving or deep running lure

TROLLING RIGS

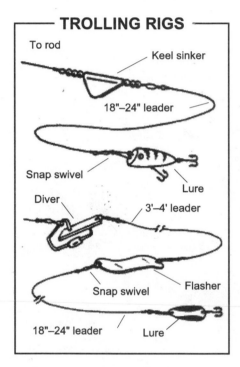

To rod
Keel sinker
18"–24" leader
Snap swivel
Lure
Diver
3'–4' leader
Flasher
Snap swivel
18"–24" leader
Lure

FLY FISHING RIGS

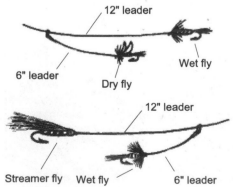

12" leader
6" leader
Wet fly
Dry fly

12" leader
Streamer fly   Wet fly   6" leader

SPINNING RIGS

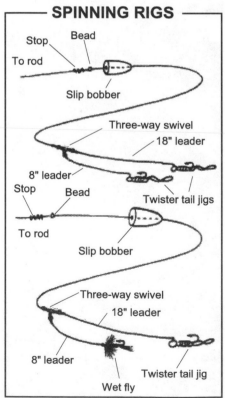

Stop   Bead
To rod
Slip bobber

Three-way swivel
18" leader
8" leader
Stop   Bead
Twister tail jigs

To rod
Slip bobber

Three-way swivel
18" leader
8" leader
Wet fly
Twister tail jig

Fishing Rigs

The following illustrations show a few of the many rigs used for bottom or still fishing.

— STILL FISHING —

These rigs could be used to keep the bait off the bottom or at a predetermined depth. Rigs #1 and #2 can also be used without bobbers for bottom fishing. Rig #3, which is a crappie rig, can also be used for other types of fish.

— BOTTOM FISHING —

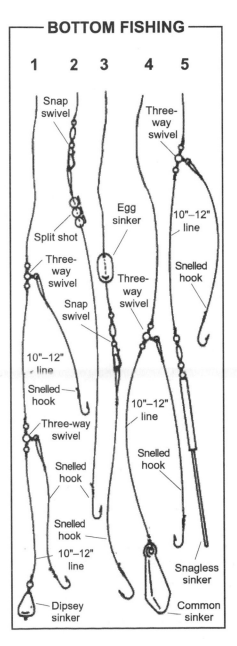

1   2   3   4   5

Snap swivel

Three-way swivel

Split shot

Egg sinker

Three-way swivel

10"–12" line

Snelled hook

Snap swivel

Three-way swivel

10"–12" line

Three-way swivel

Snelled hook

10"–12" line

Snelled hook

Snelled hook

10"–12" line

Snelled hook

Dipsey sinker

Snagless sinker

Common sinker

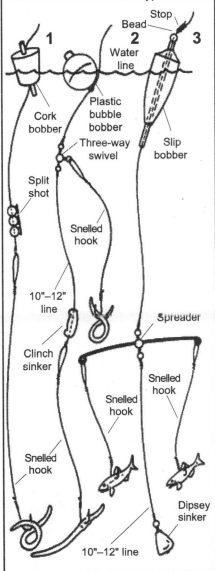

Stop

Bead

1   2   3

Water line

Cork bobber

Plastic bubble bobber

Three-way swivel

Slip bobber

Split shot

Snelled hook

10"–12" line

Clinch sinker

Spreader

Snelled hook

Snelled hook

Snelled hook

10"–12" line

Dipsey sinker

LINDY RIG

The Lindy rig is a simple, effective way to present a minnow, leech, or nightcrawler so that it appears as alive and natural as possible. It's easy to rig, and a sure-fire method to use when walleye fishing.

The following illustrations show how to set up the Lindy rig, which can be fished by trolling, back trolling, drift fishing, anchoring and casting, or still fishing.

STEP 1
Let out a few feet of line.

STEP 2
Push the line through the Lindy sinker, making sure the heavy end is toward the hook.

STEP 3
Tie your line to one end of a barrel swivel.

STEP 4
Tie an 8 lb. test, 36" long mono leader to the other end of the swivel.

STEP 5
Slip a small adjustable type of float (optional) onto the leader and tie on a #8 or #10 hook.

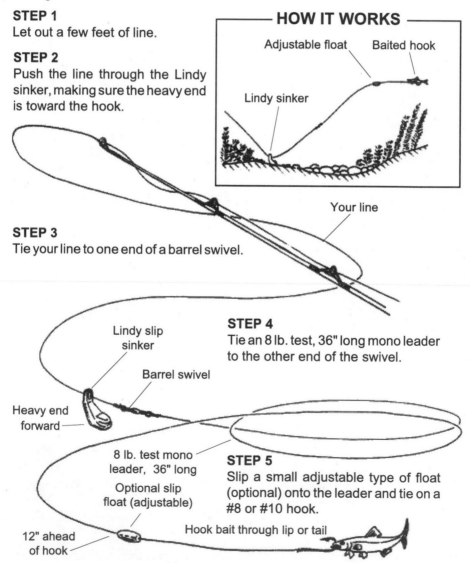

HOW IT WORKS

Adjustable float   Baited hook

Lindy sinker

Your line

Lindy slip sinker

Barrel swivel

Heavy end forward

8 lb. test mono leader, 36" long

Optional slip float (adjustable)

12" ahead of hook

Hook bait through lip or tail

LINDY RIG VARIATIONS

The following illustrations show various ways to change the basic Lindy rig for specific fishing conditions.

── FLOATING RIG ──

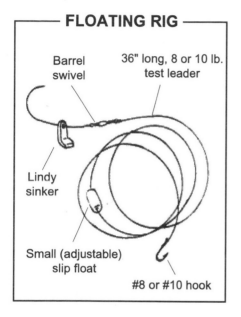

Barrel swivel

36" long, 8 or 10 lb. test leader

Lindy sinker

Small (adjustable) slip float

#8 or #10 hook

── SPLIT SHOT RIG ──

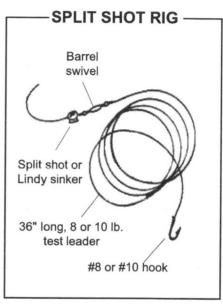

Barrel swivel

Split shot or Lindy sinker

36" long, 8 or 10 lb. test leader

#8 or #10 hook

── WEEDLESS RIG ──

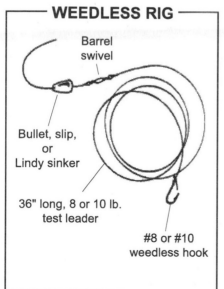

Barrel swivel

Bullet, slip, or Lindy sinker

36" long, 8 or 10 lb. test leader

#8 or #10 weedless hook

── OFF-BOTTOM RIG ──

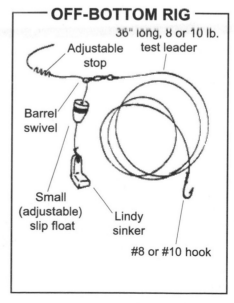

36" long, 8 or 10 lb. test leader

Adjustable stop

Barrel swivel

Small (adjustable) slip float

Lindy sinker

#8 or #10 hook

GREAT LAKES TROLLING RIG

The following illustrations show how to set up a trolling rig for salmon or trout fishing in the Great Lakes region and how it works.

Diver sinkers such as the Oregon, Pink Lady, and Deep Six are used to pull the lure or bait down to the desired depth (the faster the trolling speed, the deeper it dives). In addition, a metal blade, called a flasher or dodger, is also attached between the diver sinker and the lure to give the lure or bait more action while it is being pulled through the water.

DIVER: HOW IT WORKS

DIVING POSITION

To rod

Sliding barrel swivel

To lure

Diver (adjustable weight)

RETRIEVING POSITION

To rod   Diver   To lure

Swivel slides forward on diver when tipped by fish strike.

Line to rod

Diving sinker

Line from the sinker to the flasher or dodger should be 34" long, 15 to 20 lb. test.

Line from the flasher or dodger to the lure or bait should be 18" long and 10 to 12 lb. test.

Flasher or dodger

FLASHER/DODGER: HOW IT WORKS

Flasher/dodger causes lure or bait to swing from side to side.

Snap swivel

Lure or bait

TROLLING RIGS FOR SALMON AND TROUT

Shown below are just a few of the more popular rigs used for trolling in both deep and shallow waters during the spring, fall, or summer for trout or salmon in the Great Lakes region.

VARIOUS TYPES OF RIGS

SPRING/FALL — SHALLOW WATER RIGS

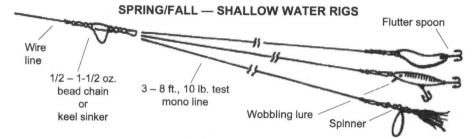

Flutter spoon

Wire line

1/2 – 1-1/2 oz.
bead chain
or
keel sinker

3 – 8 ft., 10 lb. test
mono line

Wobbling lure

Spinner

SUMMER — DEEP WATER RIGS — FISH ON THE BOTTOM

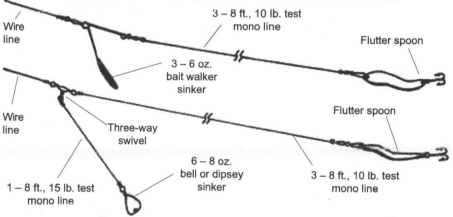

Wire line

3 – 8 ft., 10 lb. test
mono line

Flutter spoon

3 – 6 oz.
bait walker
sinker

Flutter spoon

Wire line

Three-way
swivel

6 – 8 oz.
bell or dipsey
sinker

3 – 8 ft., 10 lb. test
mono line

1 – 8 ft., 15 lb. test
mono line

SUMMER — DEEP WATER RIGS — FISH OFF THE BOTTOM

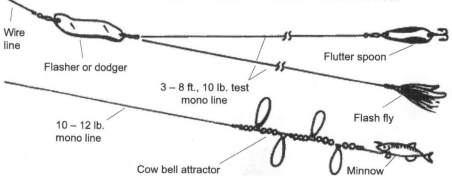

Wire line

Flasher or dodger

Flutter spoon

3 – 8 ft., 10 lb. test
mono line

Flash fly

10 – 12 lb.
mono line

Cow bell attractor

Minnow

WOLF RIVER RIG

The Wolf River rig was developed for walleye and white bass fishing during the annual spring runs on the famous Wolf River in central Wisconsin. The rig is designed for fishing in fast river currents, keeping the bait 12 inches above the bottom.

The following illustrations show how to set up a Wolf River rig and how it works.

STEP 1
Let out a few feet of line.

STEP 2
Tie a three-way swivel onto the line.

STEP 3
Tie an 8 lb. test, 24" long mono leader with a #8 or #10 hook onto the opposite eye of the three-way swivel.

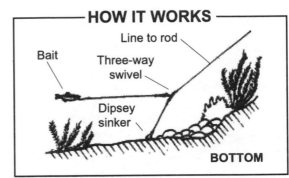

HOW IT WORKS

Line to rod

Bait

Three-way swivel

Dipsey sinker

BOTTOM

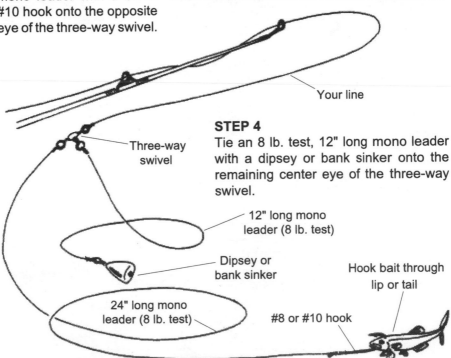

Your line

Three-way swivel

STEP 4
Tie an 8 lb. test, 12" long mono leader with a dipsey or bank sinker onto the remaining center eye of the three-way swivel.

12" long mono leader (8 lb. test)

Dipsey or bank sinker

24" long mono leader (8 lb. test)

Hook bait through lip or tail

#8 or #10 hook

PLASTIC WORM RIGS

The following illustrations are examples of various ways to rig a plastic worm. Some of the examples are named after the specific part of the country where they originated.

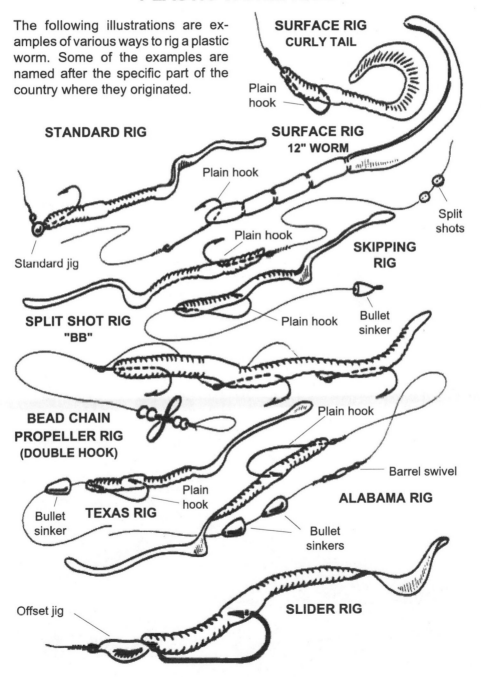

SURFACE RIG CURLY TAIL

Plain hook

STANDARD RIG

Standard jig

SURFACE RIG 12" WORM

Plain hook

Plain hook

Split shots

SKIPPING RIG

SPLIT SHOT RIG "BB"

Plain hook

Bullet sinker

BEAD CHAIN PROPELLER RIG (DOUBLE HOOK)

Plain hook

Barrel swivel

ALABAMA RIG

Bullet sinker

TEXAS RIG

Plain hook

Bullet sinkers

Offset jig

SLIDER RIG

LIVE BAIT RIGS
BASS

The following illustrations show the most deadly live bait rigs to use when fishing for largemouth and smallmouth bass.

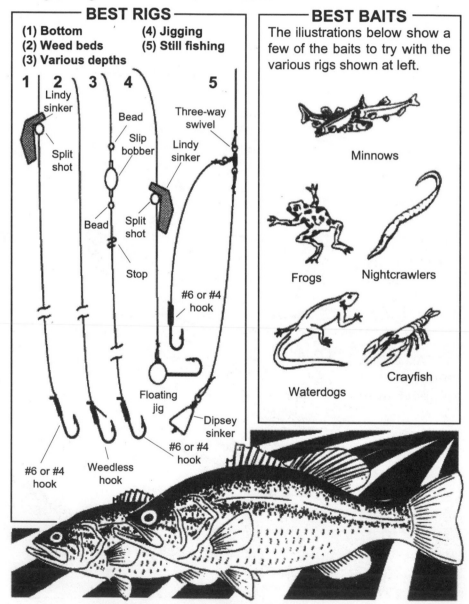

BEST RIGS

(1) Bottom
(2) Weed beds
(3) Various depths
(4) Jigging
(5) Still fishing

1

2
Lindy sinker
Split shot
#6 or #4 hook

3
Bead
Bead
Weedless hook

4
Slip bobber
Split shot
Stop
Floating jig
#6 or #4 hook

5
Three-way swivel
Lindy sinker
#6 or #4 hook
Dipsey sinker

BEST BAITS

The illustrations below show a few of the baits to try with the various rigs shown at left.

Minnows

Frogs   Nightcrawlers

Waterdogs

Crayfish

BLUEGILLS

The following illustrations show the most deadly live bait rigs to use when fishing for bluegills.

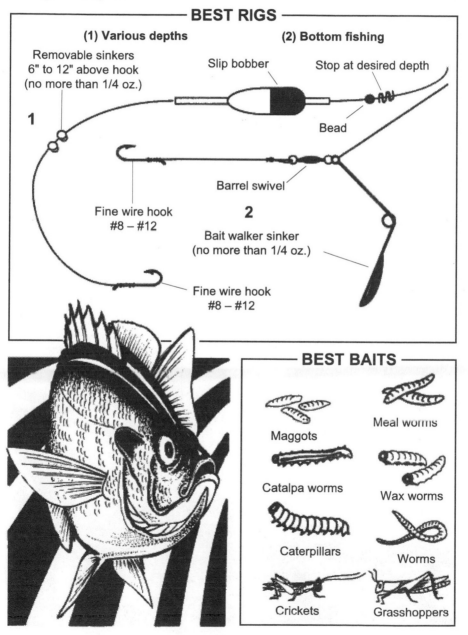

── BEST RIGS ──

(1) Various depths

Removable sinkers
6" to 12" above hook
(no more than 1/4 oz.)

1

Fine wire hook
#8 – #12

Fine wire hook
#8 – #12

(2) Bottom fishing

Slip bobber

Stop at desired depth

Bead

Barrel swivel

2

Bait walker sinker
(no more than 1/4 oz.)

── BEST BAITS ──

Maggots

Meal worms

Catalpa worms

Wax worms

Caterpillars

Worms

Crickets

Grasshoppers

CRAPPIES

The following illustrations show the most deadly live bait rigs to use when fishing for crappie.

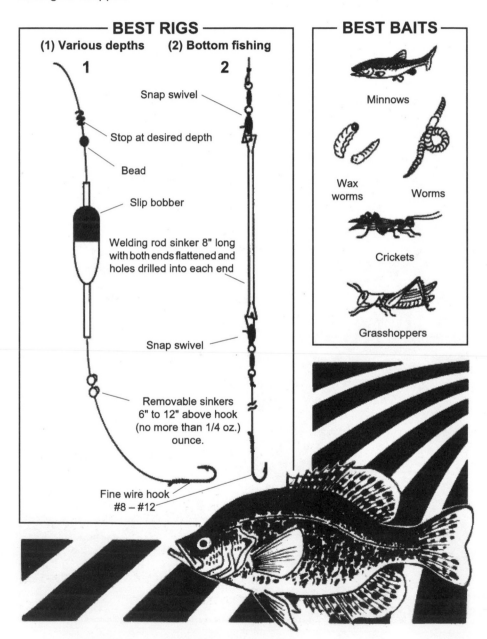

─── BEST RIGS ───

(1) Various depths   (2) Bottom fishing

1   **2**

Snap swivel

Stop at desired depth

Bead

Slip bobber

Welding rod sinker 8" long with both ends flattened and holes drilled into each end

Snap swivel

Removable sinkers 6" to 12" above hook (no more than 1/4 oz.) ounce.

Fine wire hook #8 – #12

─── BEST BAITS ───

Minnows

Wax worms   Worms

Crickets

Grasshoppers

MUSKIE

The following illustrations show the most deadly live bait rigs to use when fishing for muskie.

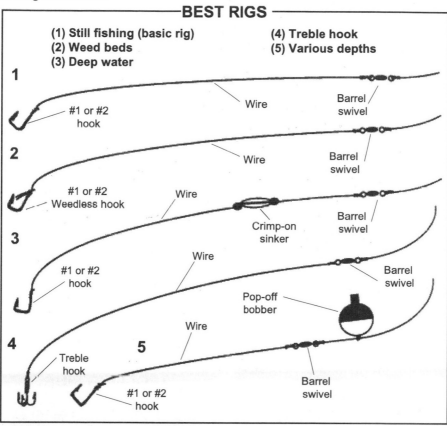

─── **BEST RIGS** ───

(1) Still fishing (basic rig)   **(4) Treble hook**
(2) Weed beds   **(5) Various depths**
(3) Deep water

1

Wire   Barrel swivel

#1 or #2 hook

2

Wire   Barrel swivel

#1 or #2 Weedless hook

Wire

3

Crimp-on sinker   Barrel swivel

#1 or #2 hook

Wire   Barrel swivel

Pop-off bobber

Wire

4   **5**

Treble hook

Barrel swivel

#1 or #2 hook

Barrel swivel

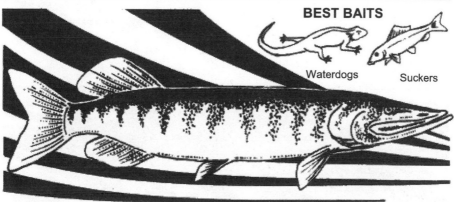

BEST BAITS

Waterdogs   Suckers

NORTHERN PIKE

The following illustrations show the most deadly live bait rigs to use when fishing for northern pike.

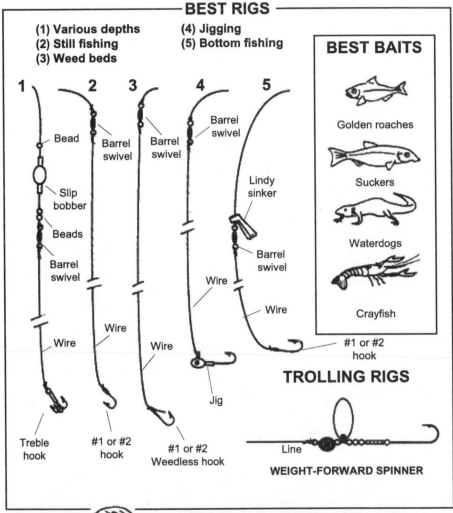

BEST RIGS

(1) **Various depths**
(2) **Still fishing**
(3) **Weed beds**
(4) **Jigging**
(5) **Bottom fishing**

BEST BAITS

Golden roaches

Suckers

Waterdogs

Crayfish

1

Bead

Slip bobber

Beads

Barrel swivel

Wire

Treble hook

2

Barrel swivel

Wire

#1 or #2 hook

3

Barrel swivel

Wire

#1 or #2 Weedless hook

4

Barrel swivel

Wire

Jig

5

Barrel swivel

Lindy sinker

Barrel swivel

Wire

Wire

#1 or #2 hook

TROLLING RIGS

Line

WEIGHT-FORWARD SPINNER

WALLEYE AND SAUGER

The following illustrations show the most deadly live bait rigs to use when fishing for walleye or sauger.

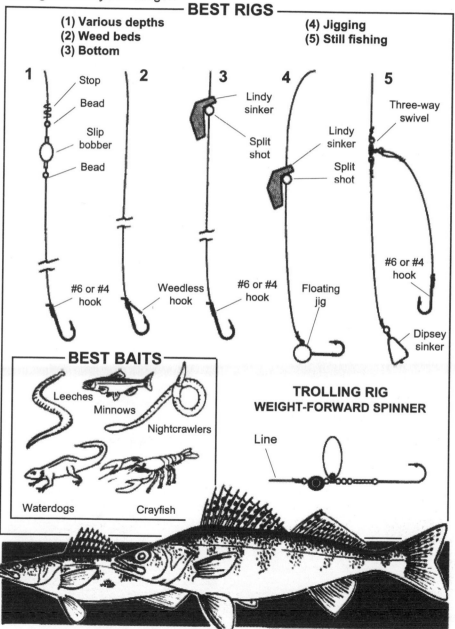

BEST RIGS

(1) Various depths
(2) Weed beds
(3) Bottom

(4) Jigging
(5) Still fishing

1
Stop
Bead
Slip bobber
Bead
#6 or #4 hook

2
Weedless hook

3
Lindy sinker
Split shot
#6 or #4 hook

4
Lindy sinker
Split shot
Floating jig

5
Three-way swivel
#6 or #4 hook
Dipsey sinker

BEST BAITS

Leeches
Minnows
Nightcrawlers
Waterdogs
Crayfish

TROLLING RIG
WEIGHT-FORWARD SPINNER

Line

DEAD BAIT RIG
PIKE AND MUSKIE

Dead bait fishing is a common practice in many areas of the country, due to the fact that most bait fish have an average life expectancy of five years, at which time they die off and sink to the bottom, becoming easy food for a variety of species. Both the pike and muskie are accustomed to feeding on these dead fish, which give off an oily scent that attracts predators from great distances.

The following illustrations show how to make a dead bait rig using suckers or large chubs as bait for pike or muskie fishing.

── DEAD BAIT RIG ──

STEP 1
Take a 12" piece of wire leader material and slip one end through a #4 treble hook. Then slip both ends through a connector sleeve, forming a 1" loop above the hook, and crimp the sleeve.

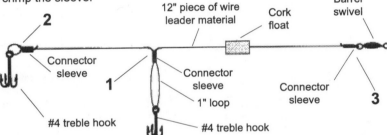

STEP 2
Take one of the free ends of the leader material and slip on a second connector sleeve and another treble hook. Slip the wire material back into the connector sleeve, snug it up close to the hook, and crimp the connector sleeve as shown in the illustration.

STEP 3
On the opposite end of the leader material, slip on the cork float, a third connector sleeve, and a barrel swivel. Pass the loose end back into the connector sleeve, snug it up close to the barrel swivel, and again crimp the sleeve.

RIGGING

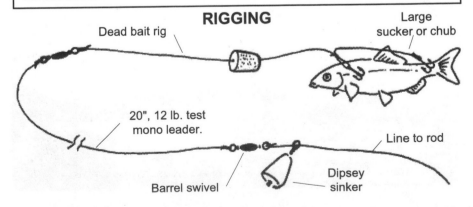

76

DROPPER RIGS
STREAM AND RIVER FISHING

Dropper rigs are used basically during early spring conditions when fishing rivers or streams. They are used to keep the bait near the bottom, using the river's or stream's current. The length of the leader to the hook is critical in keeping the bait off the bottom.

Dropper rigs can be used for a variety of species, such as trout, steelhead, walleye, or most any species found in rivers or streams.

COLD WATER CONDITIONS (Early Spring)

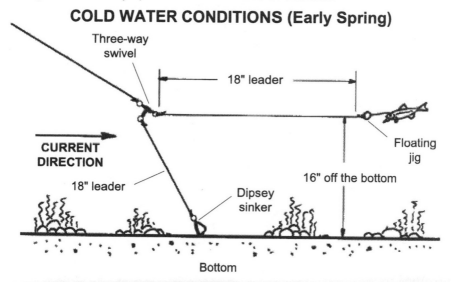

WARMING WATER CONDITIONS (Late Spring)

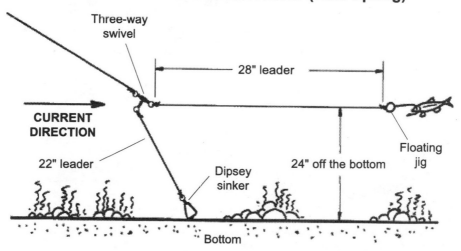

CASTING BUBBLE RIGS

The casting bubble rig is used to cast ultra-light flies using a spinning outfit rather than a fly rod. If you don't know how to handle a fly rod, the casting bubble rig will allow you to cast any of the small flies (such as nymphs or wets) or larger flies (such as streamers or buck tails) great distances. Casting bubbles can be purchased in most bait shops or sporting goods stores.

The casting distance and the fishing depth can also be controlled with some of the various types of rigs, depending on the amount of water added to the bubble. The following illustration shows the proper ways to rig casting bubbles.

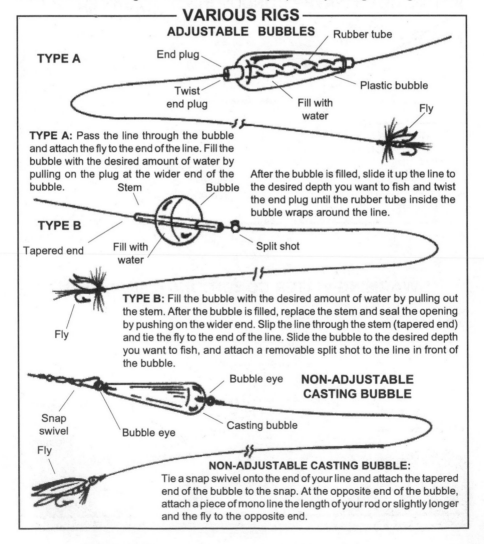

VARIOUS RIGS

ADJUSTABLE BUBBLES

TYPE A

End plug · Rubber tube · Twist end plug · Plastic bubble · Fill with water · Fly

TYPE A: Pass the line through the bubble and attach the fly to the end of the line. Fill the bubble with the desired amount of water by pulling on the plug at the wider end of the bubble.

After the bubble is filled, slide it up the line to the desired depth you want to fish and twist the end plug until the rubber tube inside the bubble wraps around the line.

TYPE B

Stem · Bubble · Tapered end · Fill with water · Split shot · Fly

TYPE B: Fill the bubble with the desired amount of water by pulling out the stem. After the bubble is filled, replace the stem and seal the opening by pushing on the wider end. Slip the line through the stem (tapered end) and tie the fly to the end of the line. Slide the bubble to the desired depth you want to fish, and attach a removable split shot to the line in front of the bubble.

NON-ADJUSTABLE CASTING BUBBLE

Bubble eye · Snap swivel · Bubble eye · Casting bubble · Fly

NON-ADJUSTABLE CASTING BUBBLE:
Tie a snap swivel onto the end of your line and attach the tapered end of the bubble to the snap. At the opposite end of the bubble, attach a piece of mono line the length of your rod or slightly longer and the fly to the opposite end.

Chapter 6

WHEN TO FISH

EARLY SEASON FISHING

After the first warming trends of spring, just after ice-out (in March or April), try some of the following tips.

WHEN TO FISH

The time of day for early season fishing is critical for the best results. The following illustrations can be used as a general rule.

EARLY MORNING:
6:00 – 9:00 A.M.

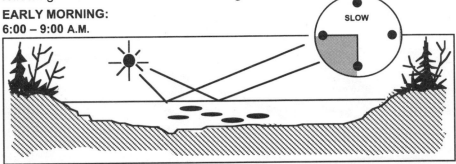

Cool water temperature and low angle of the sun's rays, which bounce off the water, provide little action.

LATE MORNING TO EARLY AFTERNOON:
9:00 A.M. – 1:00 P.M.

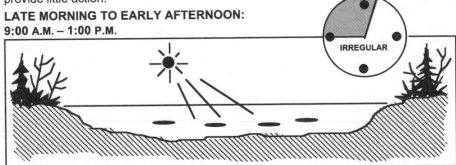

Sun starts to penetrate water, surface starts to warm up. Often produces, but could be irregular.

AFTERNOON TO EARLY DUSK:
1:00 – 5:00 P.M.

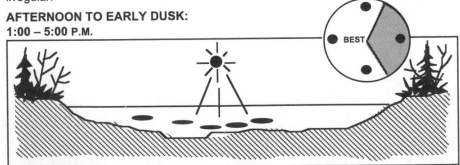

Sun's rays at maximum penetration. Best time to fish, when air and water temperatures are warmest.

COLD FRONTS

During the early season, cold fronts are one of the key factors that will affect fishing. After a warming trend has set in for a few days and a cold front approaches, the effects of the front are usually as follows:

**First day
of warming trend**

Excellent fishing for a couple of hours during the warmest part of the day.	**1:00 to 3:00 P.M.**

**Second day
of warming trend**

Excellent fishing same as first day except for a longer period of time.	**12:00 to 4:00 P.M.**

**Third day
of warming trend**

Good fishing in the late morning as well as in the afternoon.	**9:00 A.M. to 4:00 P.M.**

**Fourth day –
Cold front to hit mid-day**

Excellent fishing during the period before the cold front hits.	**8:00 A.M. to mid-day**

After the cold front hits, fishing will drop off or come to a complete stop. The cycle will repeat itself with the next warming trend and keep repeating until the spring turnover of the lake water.

Knowing where to fish after early season ice-out can be determined by using a little common sense. Consider the following factors when selecting the water you plan to fish.

BEST PLACES

- **SMALL LAKES**
- **PONDS**
- **QUARRIES**

BEST WATER

Remember, darker bottom areas such as mud flats and shallow, silt-covered areas absorb heat and warm up quicker than light-bottomed areas such as sand or gravel. Most early season fish will seek out the warmest water.

HOW TO FISH

Smaller lures or live baits will generally produce best in early spring, as will a slow-to-medium retrieve.

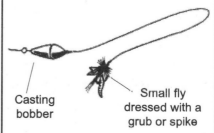

Casting bobber

Small fly dressed with a grub or spike

MID-SEASON FISHING

Here are just a few tips to try during the summer months (mid-June through mid-September) when the fishing slows down.

WHEN TO FISH

During the summer, as a general rule, early morning and late evening are the best times to fish.

EARLY MORNING: 4:30 to 9:00 A.M.

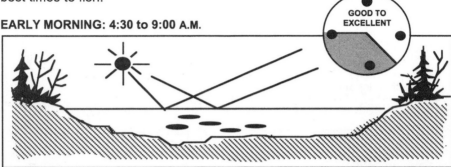

Fish are active just before daybreak (4:30 A.M.) up to about 9:00 A.M. Fishing will be excellent.

**MID-MORNING TO LATE AFTERNOON:
9:00 A.M. to 5:00 P.M.**

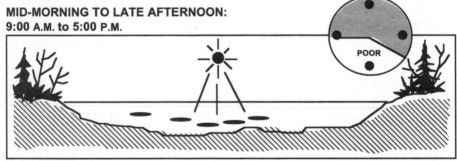

Fish are inactive during most of the day (9:00 A.M. to 5:00 P.M.). Most species will be in deep water.

**SUNSET TO EARLY EVENING:
6:00 P.M. to 9:00 P.M.**

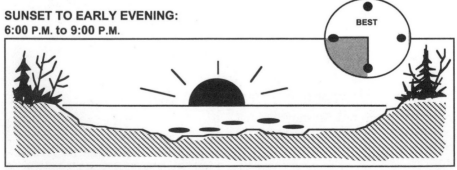

Fish are again active when the sun starts to set (6:00 P.M. to 9:00 P.M.). Excellent fishing.

When to Fish

During the summer months, fish are harder to catch for two main reasons.

1. THE FOOD CHAIN IS AT ITS PEAK.

Fish become very selective. They feed less often, but gorge themselves when they do start feeding.

2. FISH ARE HARDER TO FIND DUE TO ABUNDANT COVER.

Weed growth is at its maximum in the summer, and most predators hide in ambush in the weed beds or at their edges. They also use them as resting places between feeding sprees.

SUMMER STAGNATION

During mid-season, most lakes go through what is called the summer stagnation cycle. The surface water warms to well over 39.2° F. and floats on the heavier water below. Most lakes stratify into three layers, as shown below. The top layer is the warmest, the second is cooler and the third is cold and low in oxygen. Most fish species prefer the middle layer, but they all venture into the upper layer during feeding sprees.

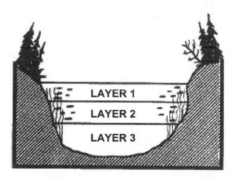

WIND EFFECT

Wind can matter during the hot days of mid-season fishing. Strong winds can push cooler offshore water close in to shore, bringing in bait fish and predators to feed. The bait fish will be attracted to insects blown into the water by the wind, which in turn will attract the larger predators.

The next time you're tempted to fish the calm side of the lake where you may be more comfortable, remember that you may have better luck on the windy side.

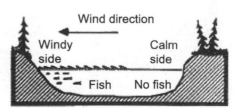

LATE SEASON FISHING

The following are just a few tips to try during the fall months (late September through ice-up), when the fall turnover is in process.

WHEN TO FISH

Water temperature is the most important factor to consider during this period. Daylight hours are shorter, limiting the warming effects of the sun. Conditions will be similar to early spring fishing. As a general rule, most fish will be scattered throughout the lake, feeding near the surface.

EARLY MORNING:
DAYBREAK TO 9:00 A.M.

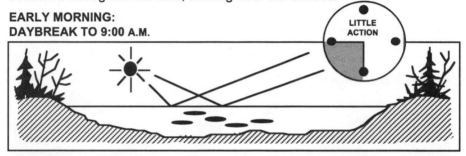

Cool water temperature and little sun penetration into water results in poor action.

LATE MORNING:
9:00 A.M. TO NOON

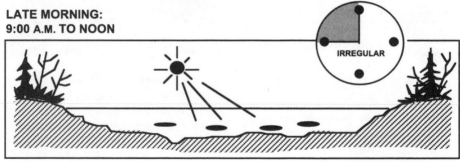

Fish are active in shallow warmer water. Often produces, but fishing is irregular.

AFTERNOON TO EVENING:
12:00 P.M. TO 6:00 P.M.

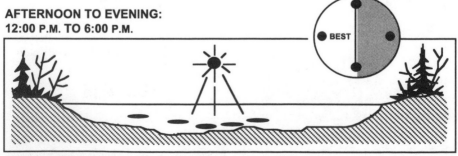

Surface waters are the warmest, and fish are active, including deep water species. Best fishing.

During the fall season, fish become more active. They feed more often and migrate away from their summer haunts.

CONCENTRATIONS OF BAIT FISH

To find active fish consistently in the fall, fish areas having concentrations of bait fish.

WARMEST WATER

Heat from the sun will be the single most important factor that governs fish activity on most lakes in the fall. Fish will seek the warmer surface waters or the shallows.

FALL TURNOVER

During the fall season, the surface water cools until it becomes heavier than the water beneath it. It sinks and mixes with the deeper water until all the water has the same temperature. This process will continue until ice-up and most fish will be scattered throughout the lake, feeding near the surface.

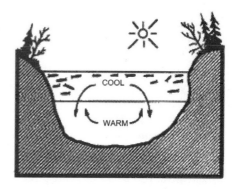

BEST WATERS

As is true in the spring, darker bottom areas such as mud flats or silt-covered areas will attract more fish because they absorb heat and warm the water around them.

During the late fall season, fish continue to feed much better in very clear water.

When fishing around the time of fall turnover, be willing to change lakes. Some lakes have longer turnover periods than others.

SEASONAL TIPS ON PRESENTATION

The way in which you present your lure or bait during the various seasons can be an important factor. Presentation can be defined as the way you display your bait or lure to a fish. It can include depth, size, color, speed, and action. With each of these factors in mind, consider the following tips to improve your ability to catch fish.

DEPTH

Try the bottom, disturbing it with your bait or lure. Bounce it along, and if that doesn't work, raise it off the bottom and jig it. Vary your depth until you locate the fish. Fish can be found suspended over holes or other forms of structure during any season.

SIZE

Choose the proper size lures for the type of fish you're after. During early spring, smaller lures are more effective.

COLOR

An old rule that's been around for ages regarding color is the one about dark lures on dark days and bright lures on bright days. There may be some truth to the rule, but water clarity should be the most important deciding factor when selecting the color of the lure to be used.

In dirty water, most fish feed by sound or smell because visibility is limited. Brightly colored lures that generate some form of sound would be the most productive under these conditions. In clear water, where visibility is good, bright lures that can be seen readily are your best bet.

SPEED

Another old rule is the one about how fast you retrieve a lure in the early spring.

The rule says "a slow or medium retrieve is the most productive" because in the early spring, when the water is cold, the fish are less active. In most cases this is true, but it's a good practice to vary your retrieves until you discover the one that's the most effective regardless of the season.

ACTION

Another important factor to consider is the action of your bait or lure. All lures represent some type of food on which fish feed. The lure's movement through the water attracts the fish. Try stop-and-go movements, short jerks, side-to-side movements, and the like.

STOP-AND-GO

SHORT JERKS

SIDE-TO-SIDE
(Top view)

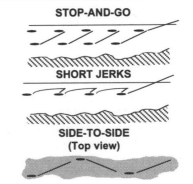

SEASONAL LAKE TURNOVERS

A body of water goes through an annual cycle of temperature changes paralleling the seasons. Knowing what the water conditions are and how they affect the fish during each season change can improve your chances of a better catch. The following illustrations depict each season change and the effects on the fish.

SPRING TURNOVER

After ice-out, surface water warms from 32° F to its maximum density at 39° F. The heavier surface waters then sink and mix with the deeper, lighter waters. As the stagnant deep water reaches the surface, it is charged with oxygen by the spring winds and warmed by the sun, repeating the cycle until the water temperature is uniform throughout the lake.

Most fish will be found in the shallower areas of the lake where the waters warm more quickly.

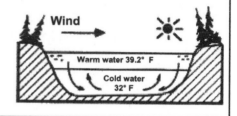

SUMMER STAGNATION

During the summer, surface water warms and rapidly becomes less dense than the water below it. It floats on top of the colder water throughout the entire summer without mixing with the deeper waters. The upper layer of water will vary between 2 and 10 feet in depth, depending on the size of the lake.

Most fish will be found just below the warm surface band of water.

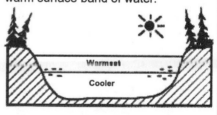

FALL TURNOVER

In the fall season, the surface water cools until it approches the temperature of the lower water beneath it. When it cools and becomes heavier, it sinks and mixes with the deeper waters until all the water has the same temperature. This process continues until the water reaches 32° F or freezes up.

During this cooling period, most fish will be scattered throughout the lake.

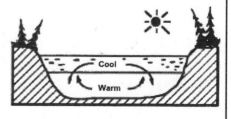

WATER TEMPERATURE

In most cases, fish activity is governed by water temperature. It affects their movements and spawning and is an important factor to consider during the various seasons. Most fish prefer a particular water temperature and seek out the depths that suit them best. Learn those depths and you'll catch more fish.

FISHING BY DEGREES

The following chart shows the temperature that specific species of fish prefer. Although you may not find the exact water temperature, most fish will be found in the water closest to the temperature listed on the chart below.

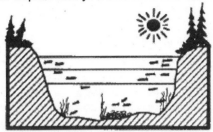

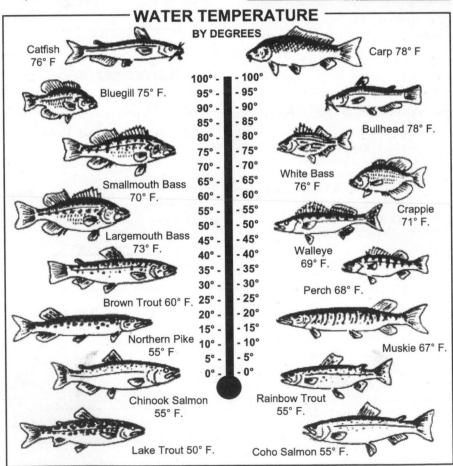

WATER TEMPERATURE
BY DEGREES

Catfish 76° F

Carp 78° F

Bluegill 75° F.

Bullhead 78° F.

White Bass 76° F

Smallmouth Bass 70° F.

Crappie 71° F.

Largemouth Bass 73° F.

Walleye 69° F.

Perch 68° F.

Brown Trout 60° F.

Northern Pike 55° F

Muskie 67° F.

Chinook Salmon 55° F.

Rainbow Trout 55° F.

Lake Trout 50° F.

Coho Salmon 55° F.

Chapter 7

WHERE TO FISH

SELECTING THE RIGHT WATER

The selection of which pond, lake, river, or stream to fish can be a determining factor in how successful or unsuccessful your fishing results will be. Before making your selection, ask yourself the following questions:

1. What season is it (spring, summer, fall, winter) and what effect will it have on the waters of my choice?

2. What are the weather conditions (cold fronts, rainy season, drought) and what effect will they have?

3. How familiar am I with the waters I plan to fish? Are they new waters that I have never fished, or waters that I have fished in the past?

4. How much time do I have to fish? Is this spot close enough to home so that I can fish it more than once, or is it so far away that I may fish it only once a year or never again?

5. What facilities are available (such as boat rentals, bait shops)? Will I be fishing from the shore or from a boat? Should I bring bait?

6. Can I get a contour map of the lake or the waters I'm planning to fish?

7. What are the water conditions (polluted, clean, clear, dirty, murky)? What effect will they have on the fish?

8. What type of fish am I after, and are they in the waters of my choice?

9. How deep are the waters I'll be fishing, and is there any structure available?

10. What time of day will I be fishing (morning, mid-day, evening), and what effect will it have on the fish?

After answering the above questions and making the necessary considerations, apply the three basic rules shown on the next page and the additional information presented in this chapter to the waters you selected, and start fishing.

FISHING BASICS

THREE BASIC RULES FOR SUCCESSFUL FISHING

1. ALWAYS FISH STRUCTURE

NO STRUCTURE

STRUCTURE

Fish underwater points, drop-offs or bars, deep edges of weed beds, sunken islands, and so forth. Also, fish artificial structure such as boat docks, piers, and fallen trees. Keep the bait near the bottom, because most fish follow structure.

REMEMBER
Most big fish stay in deep water, while most small fish stay in shallow water.

2. LEARN TO READ STRUCTURE

Get a map of the lake if you can. If you can't, look for signs of structure such as points or bars.

3. FISH WHERE THE FISH LIVE

ABRUPT CHANGE

STRUCTURE "HOME"

Drop-offs, bars, points, reefs, holes, and the like become "home" for fish. Fish the edges where the bottom has an abrupt change.

USING CONTOUR MAPS

One of the most useful things to have for locating fish is a contour map (hydrographic map) of the body of water you are planning to fish. A contour map simply indicates the various depths and irregularity of the bottom's surface using a series of lines (contour lines) that, by their relative spacing, allow you to form a mental picture of what the bottom would look like if the water was removed.

CONTOUR LINES

Lines that are close together indicate either a rise or a drop-off (which can be determined by the depth numbers); lines that are farther apart indicate a grade that is not as steep. Lines that are a long way apart indicate that the bottom is almost flat.

TYPES OF BOTTOMS

Some maps also indicate the type of bottom (mud, gravel, rock, silt) to be found in specific locations. This type of information can help you determine quickly which areas are the most likely to hold fish, and eliminate the areas that would be the least productive.

GENERAL INFORMATION

Contour maps can be obtained at most resorts, boat docks, tackle shops, or various state conservation departments. If you can't find one for the body of water in which you're interested, make your own. Sketch out the shape of the lake, and ask questions of other people who are fishing about their catches (where they were caught, how deep they fished) and mark them down. After a while, you will have a pattern for a complete contour map.

— TYPICAL CONTOUR MAP —

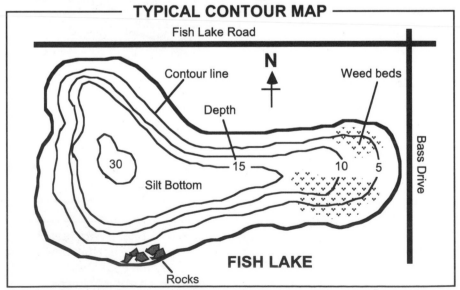

STRUCTURE FISHING
THE ANSWER TO SUCCESSFUL FISHING

Structure fishing refers to the bottom contour of a body of water, whether it is a pond, lake, stream, or river. Structure can be defined as anything unusual on the bottom of a body of water that will attract fish.

Structure can be a variety of things, such as reefs, bars, drop-offs, holes, weed beds, sunken islands, old road beds, sunken logs, or piers, but they all have one thing in common: They provide the fish with cover. Because structure provides cover, it becomes an important factor when fishing.

Most waters that are void of structure are also void of fish. If you can identify structure and fish it properly, you will improve your chances of catching more fish.

BASIC RULES FOR SUCCESS

- **ALWAYS FISH STRUCTURE**

- **LEARN TO READ STRUCTURE**

- **FISH WHERE THE FISH LIVE**

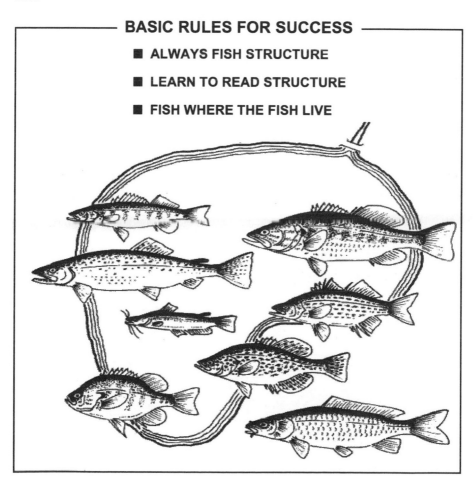

STRUCTURE FISHING TERMS

BREAK (STRUCTURE)

When the contour is no longer uniform due to a change such as drop-off, rocks, weed beds, and so on.

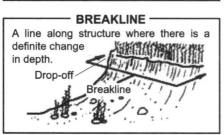

BREAKLINE

A line along structure where there is a definite change in depth.

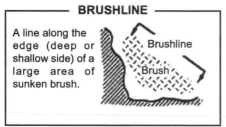

BRUSHLINE

A line along the edge (deep or shallow side) of a large area of sunken brush.

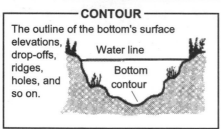

CONTOUR

The outline of the bottom's surface elevations, drop-offs, ridges, holes, and so on.

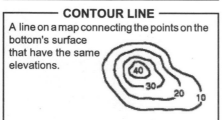

CONTOUR LINE

A line on a map connecting the points on the bottom's surface that have the same elevations.

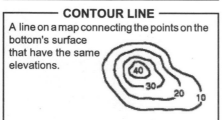

DEEP WATER

Any water that has a depth greater than 8 to 10 feet.

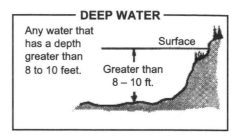

DROP-OFF

Where the contour has a rapid drop to deeper water such as a hole or channel.

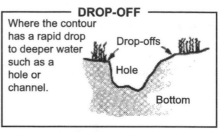

HARD BOTTOM

Bottom surface that consists of sand, clay, rocks, gravel, and so on.

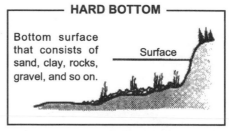

HOME

The area where fish spend most of their time; deep water or heavy cover.

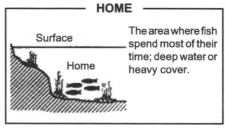

INSIDE EDGE

The shallow water edge of structure, weed beds, brush; where the cover ends toward the shoreline.

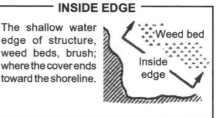

FISHING BASICS

STRUCTURE FISHING TERMS

INSIDE TURN

A cut of deeper water running into shallower water.

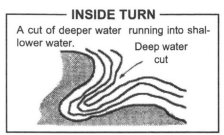

Deep water cut

RIP-RAP

Stones thrown together without order along the shoreline, extending out under the water.

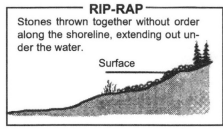

Surface

MIGRATORY ROUTE

The path fish travel from deep water to the shallows and vice versa.

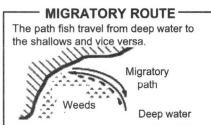

Migratory path

Weeds

Deep water

SHALLOW WATER

Any water that has a depth less than 8 feet.

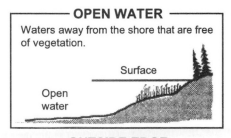

Less than 8 ft.

Surface

OPEN WATER

Waters away from the shore that are free of vegetation.

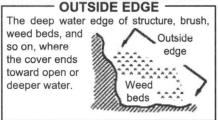

Surface

Open water

SOFT BOTTOM

Bottom surface that consists of soft silt, muck, mud, marl, and the like.

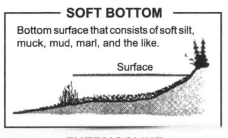

Surface

OUTSIDE EDGE

The deep water edge of structure, brush, weed beds, and so on, where the cover ends toward open or deeper water.

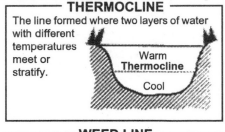

Outside edge

Weed beds

THERMOCLINE

The line formed where two layers of water with different temperatures meet or stratify.

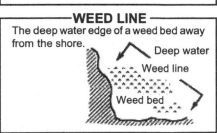

Warm
Thermocline

Cool

POINT

A tapering projection of shoreline that extends into and under the water out to deeper water.

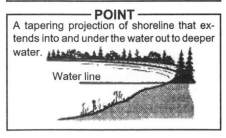

Water line

WEED LINE

The deep water edge of a weed bed away from the shore.

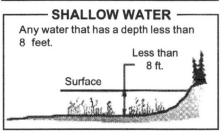

Deep water

Weed line

Weed bed

BASIC LOCATIONS

No one can predict just where the fish will be, but certain areas can be identified as preferable locations to try. Look for some of the basic locations shown in the following illustrations.

LILY PADS

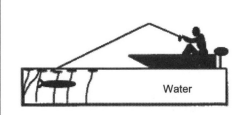

Lily pad patches provide excellent cover for a variety of fish. Work the edges and openings.

WEED BEDS

Weed beds (submerged or near shore) are also good areas to try. Fish the edges or in the beds using weedless lures.

SUBMERGED OBJECTS

Sunken trees, logs, rocks, and so on are all excellent areas to try. Cover the area from different angles.

PIERS AND DOCKS

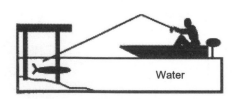

Piers and docks provide fish with shelter from the sun. Many lunkers hang around or near piers or docks. Don't pass them up.

FINDING STRUCTURE

The following examples provide a general guideline of what to look for along a shoreline if you want some clues about the structure of a pond, lake, river, or stream. Although not always true, they are a good starting point for finding fish.

——— STEEP SHORES ———

Steep shorelines indicate deep water. Fish will be found at any breakline along the walls.

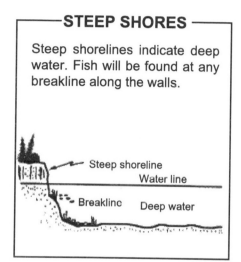

——— POINTS ———

Points along a shoreline extend under water and indicate drop-offs where fish will be located.

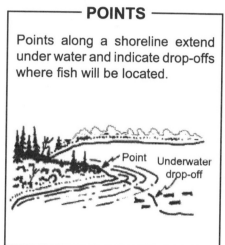

——— CREEK MOUTHS ———

Creek mouths indicate possible holes or drop-offs where fish will be located.

——— FLAT SHORES ———

Flat shorelines indicate shallow water. Fish will be away from the shore in deep water along the outside edge of weed beds or other breaklines (such as rocks, humps, and dips).

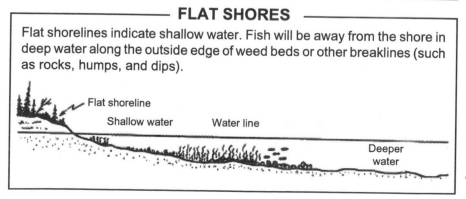

READING STRUCTURE

One thing to remember about structure fishing is that not all so-called structure found in a pond, lake, river, or stream will hold fish.

The most ideal form of structure is any irregularity on the bottom that provides fish with cover from deep water to the shallows and vice versa. Most fish will use these breaklines as their migratory routes when they leave their home (deep water) in search of food. Also remember that most fish spend most of their time in deep water (home) and move or migrate to shallower water along the breaklines provided by some form of structure, whether it is a drop-off, weed bed, sunken brush, or logs.

Important: Ideal structure will provide cover from deep water to shallow water. It must in some way tie in to the deep or deepest water in the area being fished.

A few examples of ideal and unproductive structures are shown below.

STEEP SHORE STRUCTURE

The illustrations below show two types of steep shorelines and the effect they have on attracting fish.

The first picture shows a shoreline without any type of structure, which for the most part will also be void of fish.

The second picture shows how fish relate to structure such as a rocky ledge or a breakline, which provides cover and access to deeper water.

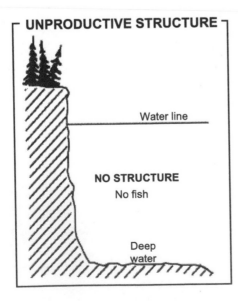

UNPRODUCTIVE STRUCTURE

Water line

NO STRUCTURE
No fish

Deep water

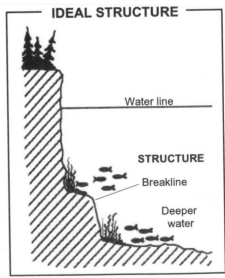

IDEAL STRUCTURE

Water line

STRUCTURE

Breakline

Deeper water

WHAT ARE BREAKLINES?

Breaklines can be defined as lines along any structure, whether it is a weed bed, brush pile, edge of a channel, a hole, or two different types of water meeting (color or temperature) where there is a definite change in the depth, either sudden or gradual. Most fish move along a breakline as a migratory route from deep water to the shallows.

POINT STRUCTURE

The following illustrations show two possible points that protrude into the water. The first point peters out before it reaches the deep water, eliminating any path or cover access for the fish from the deeper water. The second point reaches the deep water, giving the fish easy access to the shallows from the deep water along the breakline. Of the two points, the second is the best to fish and the most productive.

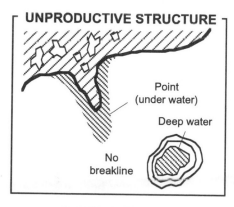

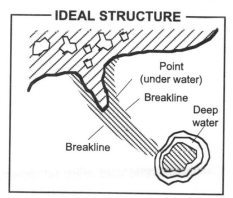

INSIDE TURNS

An inside turn is the opposite of a point. It's a cut of deep water running into shallow water along the shoreline, forming a small inlet. The sharp edges of the deep water form the breakline which will hold the fish.

Important:
Always remember, the most productive structure will provide the fish with cover from deep water (home) to shallow water. They will use the breakline as their migratory route in search of food.

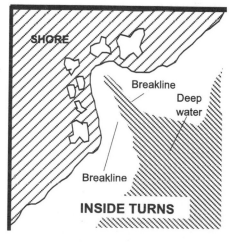

INLET OR FEEDER CREEK MOUTH STRUCTURE

The illustration to the right shows a typical inlet into a lake, river, or stream. Most inlets or feeder creeks will create a channel (structure) or what is known as a "cut" in the bottom to deeper water. Areas along the cut will hold debris (structure) washed into the main body of water from rain storms, which will attract both bait fish and predators.

The edges of the cut will be the breakline which fish will follow as their migratory route from deep water (home) to the shallows in search of food. Fish move along the channel edges and the areas where debris is concentrated, with easy access to the deeper water.

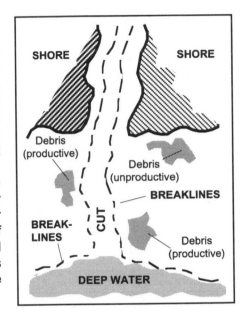

FLAT SHORE STRUCTURE

The illustration below shows a top view of a typical flat shoreline common in most lakes or reservoirs. Many locations along this type of bottom will have various forms of structure. The breakline in this type of situation will be the line formed where the depth of the water has a sudden drop.

The ideal structure, and the most productive, is the closest structure to the breakline, which provides the fish with cover from the deep water.

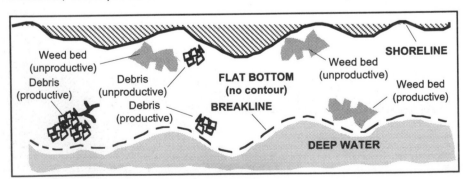

POND, LAKE, AND RESERVOIR FISHING

POND FISHING

Ponds are usually excellent fishing waters. They have abundant growth, which provides cover for bait fish as well as a variety of game fish. The game fish population in a pond can include bass, pike, pickerel, perch, panfish, and in some areas, members of the trout family. Most ponds are either creek- or spring-fed, both of which provide excellent water quality.

LAKE FISHING

Lakes vary in size, shape, and depth. They provide the same sort of food and cover for the fish population as do most ponds. They can also be fished in the same areas as a pond, and can include bass, pike, pickerel, perch, panfish, and, in some areas, trout as the principal species. Most lakes are creek-, spring-, or river-fed.

RESERVOIR FISHING

Reservoirs or impoundments also vary in size, shape, and depth. They provide the same sort of food and cover for the fish population as most lakes and ponds. They can also be fished in the same areas as a pond or lake, and can include most game fish species, depending on their location in the various parts of the country. Most reservoirs or impoundments are creek-, stream-, or river-fed.

Most ponds, lakes, and reservoirs can be fished from shore or from a boat using a variety of equipment such as spinning gear, cane poles, bait casting gear, or a fly fishing outfit.

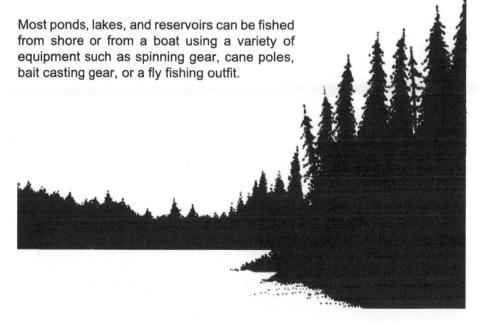

POND, LAKE, AND RESERVOIR LOCATIONS

Various areas to try in a typical pond, lake, or reservoir are described below and keyed to the illustrations on the following pages.

1. STREAM OR RIVER MOUTHS

Excellent areas to try, as incoming water brings in a variety of food that attracts both bait fish and game fish.

2. STREAM OR RIVER CHANNELS

In most ponds, lakes, or reservoirs formed by the damming of a stream or river, the original stream or river bed will have the deepest water. The deep water will be home for most fish, which will use the channel as a migratory route to and from the shallows as they search for food. The edges of the channel's breaklines formed by the original stream or river are excellent areas to try.

3. SUBMERGED ROCK PILES

In shallow water they attract spawning fish. In deep water they provide cover and are excellent areas if there is access to deeper water.

4. POINTS

Look for the point that has easy access to deep water. Fish the tip as well as corners.

5. HUMPS OR RIDGES

The edge of a hump or ridge provides excellent breaklines to fish. Shallow humps attract spawning fish in the spring. Deep humps are most productive in the summer and fall.

6. SPILLWAY OR DAM

Both above and below the spillway or dam are excellent areas to try. Some of the largest fish in a lake, pond, or reservoir lurk around the spillway.

7. DEEP HOLES OR SPRINGS

Most any of the game fish may hold along the edges of the breakline, or some species may suspend at mid-depth over the hole.

8. SUBMERGED TREE STUMPS OR FALLEN TREES

These are excellent areas depending on the amount of shade provided and access to deeper water or a breakline.

9. WEED BEDS OR LILY PADS

These areas are also excellent, depending on access to deeper water. Inside edges (shallow) are most productive in the spring or fall. Outside edges are used as a breakline or migratory route.

10. REEDS

Reeds are excellent areas in early spring for bass or pike, particularly if they connect to marshy areas or they are located at the mouth of a feeder creek.

11. OLD ROAD BEDS

Old road beds are good areas to try that provide breaklines as migratory routes to and from shallow water when fish are in search of food.

POND FISHING LOCATIONS

LAKE FISHING LOCATIONS

RESERVOIR OR IMPOUNDMENT
FISHING LOCATIONS

STREAM AND RIVER FISHING

Streams and rivers can provide excellent fishing waters if fished properly. The game fish population in a river or stream can include most any species, depending on where it's located. The most important factor to consider when fishing a river or stream is the current and the structures that affect it.

Most fish holding locations will be areas where the fast-moving water passes some form of structure, which will slow the water down and also provide cover for the fish. A few places to try are described below and illustrated on the following page.

1. DAMS OR SPILLWAYS
Both above and below the dam or spillway are excellent areas to try. Fish the rip-rap areas above the dam or spillway along the shoreline, and the first bank eddies at the base or below the dam or spillway.

2. HUMPS
Humps provide excellent staging areas for spawning walleyes and saugers during early spring. They also provide holding areas for both catfish and walleyes. Upstream humps, closest to the dam or spillway, provide the best results.

3. EDDIES
Eddies provide cover and the best potential to produce a mixed stringer of most species found in the river or stream. They can be fished from either the shore or from a boat.

4. POINTS OR BARS
Points or bars along the shoreline can be holding areas for a variety of species. They cause the current to form eddies or holes on the downstream side, which are excellent areas to try.

5. BAYS OR BACKWATERS
These are excellent areas to try during early spring. Bays and backwaters provide spawning areas for walleye, bass, and northern pike.

6. MAIN CHANNEL EDGES
Main channel edges downstream for a mile below a dam or spillway are excellent areas to try. They will hold large catfish most any time and female walleyes prior to spring spawning.

7. OUTSIDE BENDS
Outside bends along the shoreline are excellent holding areas for bass and crappies.

8. STREAM OR CREEK MOUTHS
Excellent areas to try during early spring for northern pike. They also will hold the same pike throughout the summer season.

9. BOULDERS OR ROCK PILES
Downstream sides will provide cover for a variety of species which will lie in ambush waiting for food to be washed down by the river or stream current. Fishing above the boulders or rocks and allowing the current to take your bait past the holding areas will provide the best results.

10. ISLANDS
Excellent areas to try along the sides away from the main channel. Favorite spawning areas for crappies during early spring. Also good for northern pike along the down stream points.

STREAM AND RIVER
FISHING LOCATIONS

SUMMARY

By applying everyday common sense to your fishing, you should be able to catch fish or at least improve your chances of finding them. Like anything you do, you can do it well only if you spend some time evaluating the conditions or circumstances surrounding the situation and making sound judgments to accomplish the results you're after. To succeed, you must have the facts or knowledge necessary to make your decision.

To catch fish, you must apply the same kind of thinking. You first have to find them, and to find them you need to know something about them. You need to know what affects them and you must learn to recognize their habits. Once you learn a few of these facts, you can make some judgments necessary to find and catch them.

The following list gives a few important facts that you'll need when you're trying to locate fish, regardless of the type of waters you will be fishing.

Ninety percent of all waters contain no fish.

■ ■ ■

Fish are creatures of habit; once you learn their habits,
you can find them.

■ ■ ■

Fish require some form of cover (structure)
in which to live.

■ ■ ■

Fish require some form of cover (structure) in which to move about
(migration routes) when they search for food.

■ ■ ■

Fish concentrate in areas where cover (structure)
is available.

■ ■ ■

Most game fish are in deep water most of the time
(greater than 8 or 10 feet deep).

Chapter 8

MISCELLANEOUS TIPS

LANDING YOUR CATCH

Here are a few tips on how to handle your catch after you've played it out. Don't try to land a fish until it's ready. Wait until all the fight is gone and the fish is wobbly and on its side.

EYE PICK-UP

You can lift pike, muskie, and pickerel out of the water by putting your hand over the head and grasping the fish by the eye sockets.

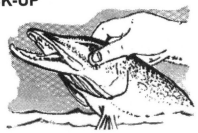

MOUTH PICK-UP

Bass or fish with small teeth can be picked up by the lower lip. This hold will paralyze the fish as long as you hang on to it. When placing your thumb in the fish's mouth, make certain that you avoid the hooks on your lure or bait.

GAFFING

When using a gaff, put it in the water under the fish and come up either under the jaw or the belly.

NET LANDING

Never scoop at the fish with the net. Hold the net in the water and lead the fish (headfirst) into it. If you miss on the first try, wait until the fish tires more or calms down, and try again.

WEIGHT

Most people who fish carry a ruler or a tape measure to measure the length of a fish, but very few carry a scale to weigh it.

If you don't have a scale, try the following chart, which is quite accurate. It can be used to determine the weight of any fish after taking a few simple measurements.

Note: *Chart is based on bass-shaped fish (800), and weights listed in the table are given in pounds.*

HOW IT WORKS

The chart shown below was compiled using the following measurements and formulas.

■ Measure the fish from the tip of the nose to the fork in the tail.

■ Then measure around the fish in front of the pectoral fins for the girth.

■ Square the girth measurement and then multiply the girth square by the length measurement.

■ Divide the sum by 800 or 900 depending on the type of fish, and the answer will give you its weight.

NO-LIE WEIGHT CHART

MEASUREMENTS

Length — Pectoral fin — Girth

Girth (inches): Around fish in front of pectoral fin.

Length (inches): Tip of nose to fork in tail.

FORMULAS

Girth x Girth = Girth squared
Girth squared x Length = Sum
Sum ÷ by ___ = Weight

Bass-shaped fish: 800
Elongated fish: 900

	10	11	12	13	14	15	16	18	20	22	24	26	28	30	32
6	0.45	0.50	0.54	0.59	0.63	0.68	0.72	0.81	0.90	0.99	1.08	X	X	X	X
7	0.61	0.67	0.74	0.80	0.86	0.92	0.98	1.10	1.23	1.35	1.47	1.59	1.72	X	X
8	0.80	0.88	0.96	1.04	1.12	1.20	1.28	1.44	1.60	1.76	1.92	2.1	2.2	2.4	2.6
9	1.01	1.11	1.22	1.32	1.42	1.52	1.62	1.82	2.0	2.2	2.4	2.6	2.8	3.0	3.2
10	1.25	1.38	1.50	1.63	1.75	1.88	2.0	2.3	2.5	2.8	3.0	3.3	3.5	3.8	4.0
11	1.51	1.66	1.82	1.97	2.1	2.3	2.4	2.7	3.0	3.3	3.6	3.9	4.2	4.5	4.8
12	1.80	1.98	2.2	2.3	2.5	2.7	2.9	3.2	3.6	4.0	4.3	4.7	5.0	5.4	5.8
13	2.1	2.3	2.5	2.7	3.0	3.2	3.4	3.8	4.2	4.6	5.1	5.5	5.9	6.3	6.8
14	2.5	2.7	2.9	3.2	3.4	3.7	3.9	4.4	4.9	5.4	5.9	6.4	6.9	7.4	7.8
15	2.8	3.1	3.4	3.7	3.9	4.2	4.5	5.1	5.6	6.2	6.8	7.3	7.9	8.4	9.0
16	3.2	3.5	3.8	4.2	4.5	4.8	5.1	5.8	6.4	7.0	7.7	8.3	9.0	9.6	10.2
17	X	4.0	4.3	4.7	5.1	5.4	5.8	6.5	7.2	7.9	8.7	9.4	10.1	10.8	11.6
18	X	X	4.9	5.3	5.7	6.1	6.5	7.3	8.1	8.9	9.7	10.5	11.3	12.2	13.0
19	X	X	X	5.9	6.3	6.8	7.2	8.1	9.0	9.9	10.8	11.7	12.6	13.5	14.4
20	X	X	X	X	7.0	7.5	8.0	9.0	10.0	11.0	12.0	13.0	14.0	15.0	16.0
22	X	X	X	X	X	9.1	9.7	10.9	12.1	13.3	14.5	15.7	16.9	18.2	19.4
24	X	X	X	X	X	X	11.5	13.0	14.4	15.8	17.3	18.7	20.2	21.6	23.0
26	X	X	X	X	X	X	X	15.2	16.9	18.6	20.3	22.0	23.7	25.4	27.0
28	X	X	X	X	X	X	X	X	19.6	21.6	23.5	25.5	27.4	29.4	31.4
30	X	X	X	X	X	X	X	X	X	24.8	27.0	29.3	31.5	33.8	36.0

CLEANING YOUR CATCH

The following steps are just a few tips on various ways to clean your catch.

PANFISH

Most panfish are less than 12" long and are difficult to fillet. Unless you are experienced at filleting fish, use the following method for panfish.

STEP 1
Hold the fish by the tail and scrape from tail to head to loosen and remove the scales, using a dull knife or a fish scraper.

Scraper

STEP 2
Cut off the head behind the pectoral fin and cut open the belly cavity.

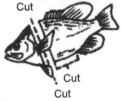

Cut

Cut

Cut

STEP 3
Remove fins by cutting into flesh on both sides and then pulling them out.

Clean out belly cavity

Pull

FILLETING

STEP 1
Cut deep on each side of dorsal fin.

STEP 2
Cut deep around head, gills, and fins.

STEP 3
Separate flesh from the rib cage.

STEP 4
Cut fillet loose.

STEP 5
Repeat steps 1 through 5 on opposite side.

STEP 6
Skin fillets by starting at tail end and inserting blade between skin and meat.

CLEANING PIKE

Many people don't like to keep pike because they consider them too bony to eat and too difficult to clean. The following illustrations show a simple method to fillet a pike and remove those pesky "Y" bones.

STEP 1

Starting with the top of the fish, cut down behind the head to the backbone. Follow the backbone back to the top rear fin and cut up and remove the piece from the fish, as shown in the illustration.

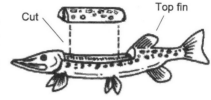

STEP 2

Next, lay the piece on its side and cut it lengthwise along the cartilago, which runs down the center of the piece (both sides).

STEP 3

Next, place the rest of the fish on its side, as shown in the illustration at right, and from the top fin (tail section), cut down through the side to the backbone and along the backbone to the tail. Repeat this step on the opposite side.

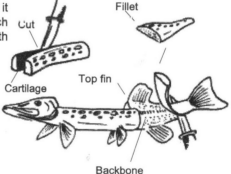

STEP 4

After removing the two tail fillets, take the remaining fish and, with the exposed backbone up, feel for the "Y" bones with your fingers (they feel like sharp needles). Slip your knife under the "Y" bones and cut carefully down to the backbone and to the back. Do the same on the opposite side.

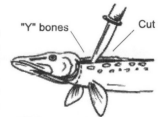

STEP 5

Next, cut down behind the gill cover to the belly and, with the tip of the knife just below the "Y" bones, cut back along the rib cage. Repeat the same on the opposite side, and also remove the two bottom fins.

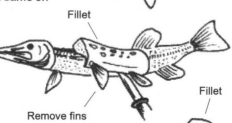

STEP 6

Take all the fillets and remove the skin by inserting the blade between the skin and meat and pulling on the skin while holding the knife in a stationary position.

CLEANING TIPS

FILET MIGNON

The cheeks are the filet mignon of the fish. When cleaning large fish, don't forget to remove these choice tidbits before you discard the head.

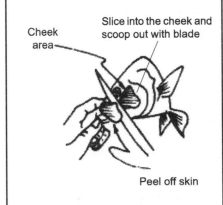

Cheek area

Slice into the cheek and scoop out with blade

Peel off skin

FISH STEAKS

Large fish like salmon can be cut into steaks rather than fillets after you gut them and remove the fins.

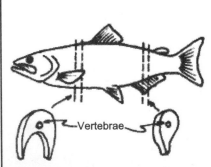

Vertebrae

Slice the steaks between the vertebrae at the desired thickness.

SKINNING CATFISH/BULLHEADS

STEP 1
Cut through the skin, completely around the head.

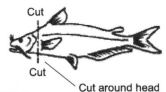

Cut

Cut

Cut around head

STEP 2
Nail head to board and peel skin back with pliers.

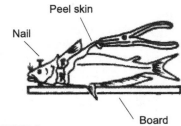

Peel skin

Nail

Board

STEP 3
After skin is peeled back, cut through the backbone behind the dorsal fin at an angle toward the head.

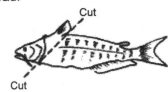

Cut

Cut

STEP 4
Break the head downwards from the body, removing the head and entrails at the same time.

Entrails

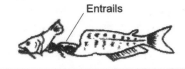

CLEANING TOOLS

If you can't find your scraper or you forget to bring it with you, try using a teaspoon or a tablespoon as a scraper. The spoon will do an excellent job, and the dull edges won't cut the fish.

── SPOON SCRAPER ──

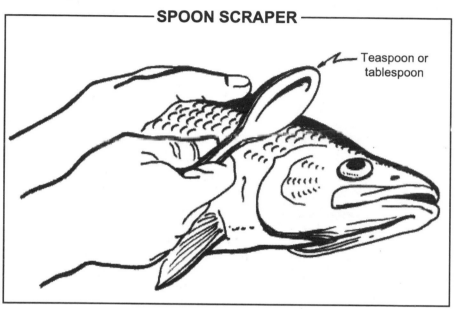

Teaspoon or tablespoon

── HOMEMADE FISH SCALER ──

All you need to make a dandy scaler are two bottle caps from a soft drink or beer bottle, a couple of screws, and a piece of wood 1" wide x 1/2" thick and 6" long.

Screw

Hole

Bottle caps

1-1/2"

3/4"

1/2"

1"

3"

6"

Cutout handle (optional)

MOUNTS

If you plan to have your fish mounted and you would like to save the meat, the following care should be taken with your catch.

—— HEAD MOUNTS ——

If you plan to have just the head mounted and eat the rest of the fish, cut the head off as shown below and freeze it as soon as possible.

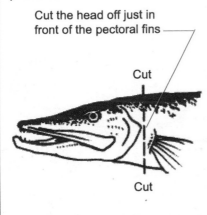

Cut the head off just in front of the pectoral fins

Cut

Cut

FULL FISH MOUNT

If you plan to have the entire fish mounted, do the following.

As soon as you can after you catch the fish, determine the best side to be displayed. This will be the "showside" and will have the least damage such as missing scales and cuts.

On the opposite side of the showside, make an incision in the center of the body, from the gill plate to about 1 inch of the tail. Make the cut deep enough so that you can get your hand into the stomach cavity. Carefully remove the stomach entrails through the cut, and wash out the cavity. Wipe the fish with a cloth to dry it as much as possible, wrap it in wax or freezer paper, and freeze it.

When you take the fish to the taxidermist, ask for the meat to be saved when the fish is skinned. Most taxidermists will be more than happy to do so.

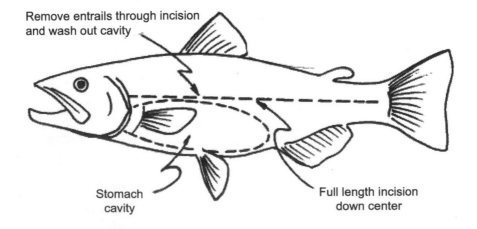

Remove entrails through incision and wash out cavity

Stomach cavity

Full length incision down center

Chapter 9

FISH IDENTIFICATION

BLUEGILL

(Lepomis macrochirus)

The bluegill is the most popular of all the panfish. It's fun to catch and is found in most lakes, rivers and streams in the eastern and midwestern parts of the United States. It is also native to some of the southern states as well as southern Canada.

The bluegill prefers weed beds with gravel or sand bottoms and is active all year long, with the spring and fall months as the peak fishing periods.

Fly fishing and still fishing are the best methods for catching this colorful little fighter, using small flies or live baits for the best results.

BEST BAITS

Some of the more popular baits to use for bluegills are shown below.

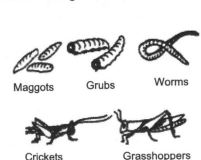

Maggots	Grubs	Worms
Crickets		Grasshoppers
Small flies	Ice spoons	Small jigs

WORLD RECORD

RECORD HOLDER: T.S. Hudson
CAUGHT: April 9, 1950
WHERE: Ketona Lake, Alabama
WEIGHT: 4 lbs., 12 oz.
LENGTH: 15"
GIRTH: 18-1/4"

Fish Identification

OTHER NAMES

Bream, Brim, Sunfish, Copper Head, Sun Perch

LIFE SPAN

The average life span of the bluegill is four to six years.

IDENTIFICATION

The most significant characteristic of the bluegill that distinguishes it from the rest of the sunfish family is the dark ear flap (without any margin) on the lower end of the gill cover. Other distinct characteristics are the bluish edges of the orange breast area and the vertical bars along the sides.

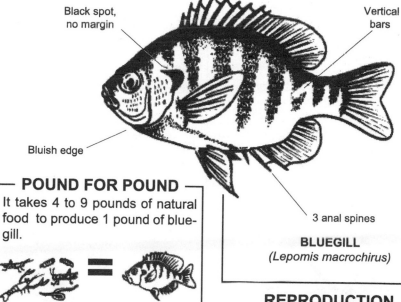

Black spot, no margin

Vertical bars

Bluish edge

3 anal spines

BLUEGILL
(Lepomis macrochirus)

POUND FOR POUND

It takes 4 to 9 pounds of natural food to produce 1 pound of bluegill.

4 to 9 lbs.   1 lb.

REPRODUCTION

Bluegills can reproduce at one year of age.

■ ■ ■ ■

They are nest builders that spawn two or three times in a year, with the male guarding the eggs and fry.

■ ■ ■ ■

A 5-inch female can lay 6,000 eggs while a 10-incher can lay over 50,000. Bluegill eggs hatch in two to five days, depending on the water temperature.

GROWTH

The average bluegill grows to about 7 inches when mature and weighs about 1/2 pound.

BOWFIN (DOGFISH)
(Amia calva)

Bowfin (dogfish) are found in most rivers, streams, lakes, ponds, and canals throughout the Mississippi basin and south Gulf States. Most often they are caught while fishing for other game fish. They inhabit sluggish waters with weedy areas and mud bottoms.

The best method to use when fishing for bowfin is a bottom rig baited with live or cut baits, but they will also take artificial lures. Once hooked, they are strong fighters that provide great sport on light tackle.

WORLD RECORD

RECORD HOLDER: Robert L. Harmon
CAUGHT: January 29, 1980
WHERE: Forest Lake, South Carolina
WEIGHT: 21 lbs., 8 oz.

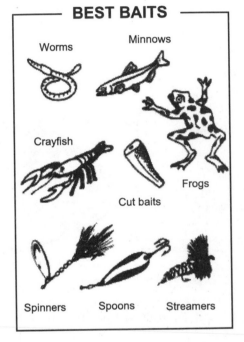

BEST BAITS

Worms

Minnows

Crayfish

Cut baits

Frogs

Spinners

Spoons

Streamers

Fish Identification

LIVING RELIC

The bowfin is a living relic from a group of primitive bony fish that lived millions of years ago.

It has a half-developed lung which allows it to tolerate water conditions with low oxygen levels. It can also survive for hours when taken out of water.

IDENTIFICATION

The bowfin is a heavy-scaled fish with a plate-like bony head and a dorsal fin that extends over most of the body length. It is a mottled olive brown color on top with a yellowish belly. The male fish has a black spot rimmed with an orange ring at the base of the upper tail fin.

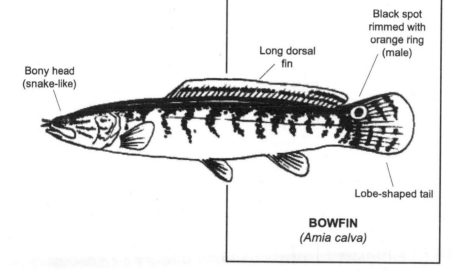

Bony head (snake-like)

Long dorsal fin

Black spot rimmed with orange ring (male)

Lobe-shaped tail

BOWFIN
(Amia calva)

REPRODUCTION

The bowfin spawns in the early spring. Spawning takes place in shallow marshy areas of lakes and streams. The male builds a nest in the muddy or sandy bottom in which the female deposits her eggs. The female can lay between 24,000 and 64,000 eggs, which hatch in eight to ten days. After laying her eggs, the female leaves the nest and the male guards the eggs or the newly hatched young until they are able to fend for themselves.

OTHER NAMES

Freshwater Dogfish, Grindle, Cypress Trout, Choupique, Cotton Fish, Scaled Ling, Mudfish

HABITAT

The bowfin prefers shallow, warm, quiet water in weedy bays, lakes, ditches, or open areas of rivers. It can tolerate stagnant water by gulping air on the surface.

BULLHEAD
(Ictaluras)

The bullhead is found in most lakes, rivers, and streams throughout the United States. It is a bottom feeder that feeds mostly at night and primarily on insects. It prefers quite sluggish waters with weedy bottoms.

Still fishing on the bottom using worms, insects, or stink baits is the best method to use when fishing for bullheads.

BEST BAITS

The following baits are just a few to try when fishing for bullheads. Live baits, as shown below, fished on the bottom produce the best results.

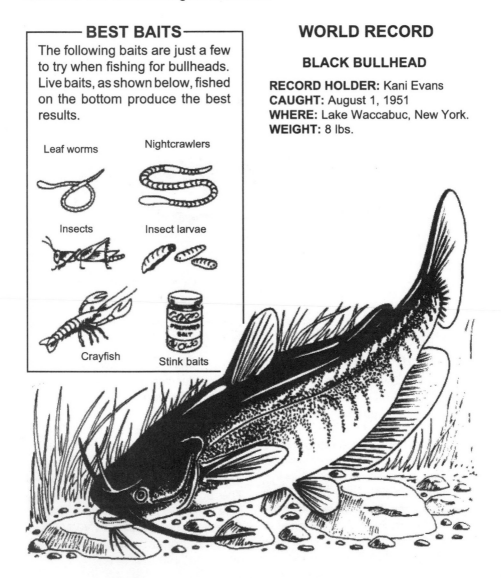

Leaf worms

Nightcrawlers

Insects

Insect larvae

Crayfish

Stink baits

WORLD RECORD

BLACK BULLHEAD

RECORD HOLDER: Kani Evans
CAUGHT: August 1, 1951
WHERE: Lake Waccabuc, New York.
WEIGHT: 8 lbs.

LIFE SPAN AND SIZE

Three species of bullheads are the most frequently caught while fishing. They are the black, brown, and yellow bullheads. They all have a life span of about four years and an average weight of 4 pounds.

IDENTIFICATON

The following illustrations show which characteristics to use to identify the three different species of bullheads.

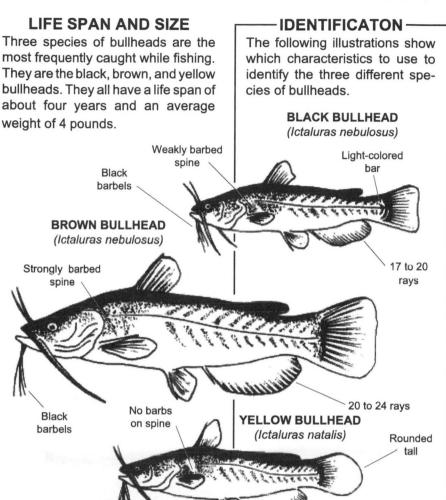

BROWN BULLHEAD
(Ictaluras nebulosus)

Weakly barbed spine

Black barbels

BLACK BULLHEAD
(Ictaluras nebulosus)

Light-colored bar

17 to 20 rays

Strongly barbed spine

Black barbels

No barbs on spine

20 to 24 rays

YELLOW BULLHEAD
(Ictaluras natalis)

Rounded tail

White barbels

24 to 27 rays

REPRODUCTION

Bullheads reach reproductive age between one and three years. They are nest builders, spawning in the spring and laying as many as 6,800 eggs. The eggs hatch in five to ten days and the young fry school together for protection In large groups, as often seen in ponds, rivers, streams, and lakes.

OTHER NAMES

BROWN BULLHEAD: Speckled Cat or Speckled Bullhead
BLACK BULLHEAD: Yellow Belly Cat or Horned Pout
YELLOW BULLHEAD: Greaser or White Whisker Bullhead

CARP
(Cyprinidae)

Carp provide sport fishing for many anglers. They are found in lakes, streams, ponds, and rivers throughout the United States. They were introduced into the United States from Europe in1879. Carp belong to the minnow family *(Cyprinidae),* which numbers about 2,000 species worldwide.

Bottom fishing with dough baits or special preparations is the best method to use when pursuing this bottom-feeding scavenger. Bow fishing in the spring during their spawning season also provides some excellent sport. They are strong fighters and will test your fishing skills on light tackle.

WORLD RECORD

RECORD HOLDER: David Nikolow
CAUGHT: June 19, 1983
WHERE: Tidal Basin, Washington, D.C.
WEIGHT: 57 lbs., 13 oz.

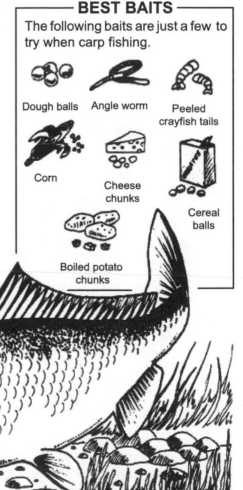

BEST BAITS

The following baits are just a few to try when carp fishing.

Dough balls   Angle worm   Peeled crayfish tails

Corn   Cheese chunks   Cereal balls

Boiled potato chunks

Fish Identification

LIFE SPAN AND SIZE

Carp have a life span of seven to eight years. The average size of a carp is about 2 to 5 pounds, but they can attain a weight of 90 pounds or better.

── IDENTIFICATION ──

Carp vary in color, from a brassy brown to a dark brassy silver. They are large, scaled fish with strong fins and spines. One of the key characteristics of the carp is its barbels, found on the sides of its mouth. The grass carp lacks the barbels, as shown below.

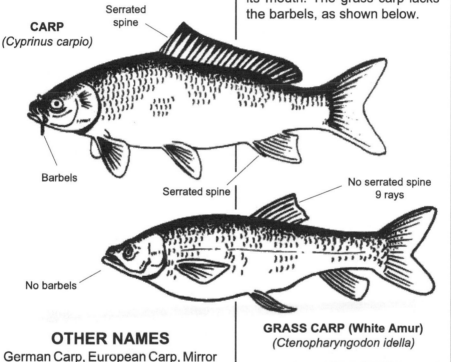

CARP
(Cyprinus carpio)

Serrated spine

Barbels

Serrated spine

No serrated spine
9 rays

No barbels

GRASS CARP (White Amur)
(Ctenopharyngodon idella)

OTHER NAMES

German Carp, European Carp, Mirror Carp, Scaleless Carp

── HABITAT ──

Certain species of carp are used for weed control in ponds and lakes.

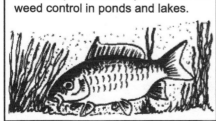

REPRODUCTION

Carp reproduce when they reach 12 inches to 15 inches in length. They spawn in the spring in the shallows by scattering their eggs. A mature female lays from 190,000 to 200,000 eggs, which hatch in about twelve days.

Carp grow to about 8 inches in their first year, then average about 1-1/2 inches of growth per year of age.

CATFISH
(Ictaluridae)

The catfish family includes twenty-four different species which are distributed in lakes, ponds, rivers, and streams throughout the United States. They are all basically bottom feeders that eat a variety of natural or specially prepared baits. Still fishing on the bottom from dusk to midnight, or again around dawn, will produce the best results. Catfish can also be taken with trot lines or artificial baits such as spoons, buck tail spinners, and small jigs dressed with minnows or worms.

WORLD RECORDS

FLATHEAD CATFISH
RECORD HOLDER: Mike Rogers
CAUGHT: March 28, 1982
WHERE: Lake Lewisville, Texas
WEIGHT: 91 lbs., 3 oz.

CHANNEL CATFISH
RECORD HOLDER: W. B. Whaley
CAUGHT: July 7, 1964
WHERE: Santee Cooper Reservoir, South Carolina
WEIGHT: 58 lbs.
LENGTH: 47-1/4"
GIRTH: 29-1/8"

BLUE CATFISH
RECORD HOLDER: Edward B. Elliot
CAUGHT: September 16, 1959
WHERE: Missouri River, South Dakota
WEIGHT: 97 lbs.
LENGTH: 57"
GIRTH: 37"

BEST BAITS
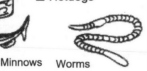

Prepared Baits
- Cheese
- Blood
- Chicken entrails
- Hotdogs

Minnows Worms

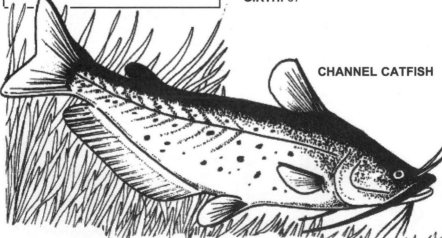

CHANNEL CATFISH

LIFE SPAN AND SIZE

The life span of a catfish ranges from eight to fifteen years depending on the species. The average size varies from 1 to 15 pounds, although certain species can exceed 100 pounds.

IDENTIFICATION

The following illustrations show three of the most frequently caught species of catfish and some of the characteristics to check for a positive identification.

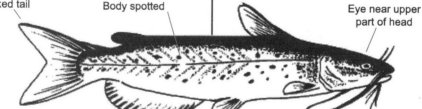

BLUE CATFISH
(Ictalurus furcatus)

Deeply forked tail

Eye near lower part of head

Straight edge

Upper lobe longer on forked tail

30 to 35 rays

Body spotted

CHANNEL CATFISH
(Ictalurus punctatus)

Eye near upper part of head

24 to 29 rays

Body mottled

FLATHEAD CATFISH
(Pylodictic olivaris)

Head greatly flattened in front, jaw protrudes

Slight fork in tail

REPRODUCTION

Catfish reproduce after they reach 12 inches in length or two years of age. They are nest builders, laying eggs in the spring that hatch in ten to twelve days.

GROWTH

The blue and flathead catfish are among the largest freshwater fish found in the United States, growing to over 100 pounds in weight.

CRAPPIE
(Pomoxis)

There are two distinct species of the crappie, the black and the white crappie. Their distribution covers most of the United States and Canada.

Spring and fall are the best times to fish for crappies, in or around dense cover such as brush piles, rocks, and weed beds.

BEST BAITS

Crappies can be caught in a variety of ways, such as fly fishing, spinning, or still fishing. They prefer live baits, but will also take artificial lures. The following examples are only a few of the many baits and lures available for crappie fishing.

LIVE BAITS

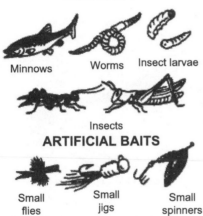

Minnows   Worms   Insect larvae

Insects

ARTIFICIAL BAITS

Small flies   Small jigs   Small spinners

CRAPPIE FACTS

The average life span of a crappie is four to five years.

■ ■ ■ ■

The average size of a crappie is 8 inches.

■ ■ ■ ■

The average weight of an adult crappie is 1-1/2 pounds, but they can reach or exceed 5 pounds.

■ ■ ■ ■

The crappie is one of the largest panfish, and also one of the finest fish for the frying pan.

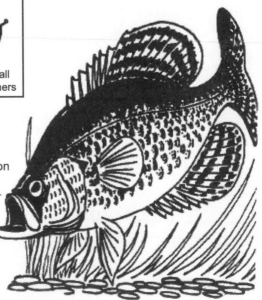

WORLD RECORDS

BLACK CRAPPIE

RECORD HOLDER: Lettie Robertson
CAUGHT: November 28, 1969
WHERE: Westwego Canal, LA
WEIGHT: 6 lbs.

WHITE CRAPPIE

RECORD HOLDER: Fred I. Bright
CAUGHT: July 31, 1957
WHERE: Enid Dam, Mississippi
WEIGHT: 5 lbs., 3 oz.

Fish Identification

OTHER NAMES

WHITE CRAPPIE:
Silver Crappie, Bachelor, Newlight

BLACK CRAPPIE:
Calico Bass, Strawberry Bass, Speckled Crappie

IDENTIFICATION

Black and white crappies are similar in appearance except for the following characteristics.

■ The markings on the sides of the black crappie are irregular, while the spots on the white crappie are vertical bars.

■ The black crappie has seven or eight dorsal spines and the white crappie has only five or six.

WHITE CRAPPIE
(Pomoxis annularis)

5 or 6 dorsal spines

7 or 8 dorsal spines

Markings irregular

Markings in vertical bars

BLACK CRAPPIE
(Pomoxis nigro-maculatus)

REPRODUCTION

The female reproductive age is two to three years for both species. They are nest builders and both spawn in the spring. The white crappie lays as many as 147,000 eggs, while the black crappie lays 180,000.

HABITAT

Both the black and the white crappie are school fish that prefer dense cover.

GAR
(Lepisosteus)

Many anglers may not consider gars as worthwhile game fish. However, after you tie into one you may not feel that way. Gars are native only to the United States and are a primitive species whose ancestors lived millions of years ago.

They can be found in many ponds, lakes, and rivers throughout the Mississippi drainage system. They are also found in the south and the southwestern states.

Still fishing with a float, wire leader, and a sharp hook using live bait is the best way to fish for them.

WORLD RECORDS

ALLIGATOR GAR

RECORD HOLDER: Bill Valverde
CAUGHT: December 2, 1951
WHERE: Rio Grande River, Texas
WEIGHT: 279 lbs.

SHORT-NOSED GAR

RECORD HOLDER: J. Pawlowski
CAUGHT: June 9, 1977
WHERE: Lake Francis Case,
      South Dakota
WEIGHT: 3 lbs., 5 oz.

─── BEST BAITS ───

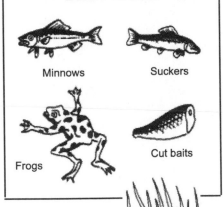

Minnows

Suckers

Frogs

Cut baits

LONG-NOSED GAR

RECORD HOLDER: T. Miller
CAUGHT: July 30, 1954
WHERE: Trinity River, Texas
WEIGHT: 50 lbs., 5 oz.

Fish Identification

LIVING RELIC

Gars are survivors of ancient fish that flourished millions of years ago. Their ancestors were around during the dinosaur age, long before most known species of modern fish came into existence.

IDENTIFICATION

The basic shape of the gar is very similar to that of the pike family members except for the mouth or beak.

The following illustrations show the different characteristics of the alligator, long-nosed, and short-nosed gars.

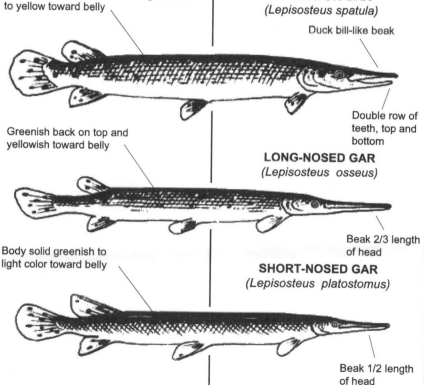

Greenish brown on back and light brown to yellow toward belly

ALLIGATOR GAR
(Lepisosteus spatula)

Duck bill-like beak

Double row of teeth, top and bottom

Greenish back on top and yellowish toward belly

LONG-NOSED GAR
(Lepisosteus osseus)

Beak 2/3 length of head

Body solid greenish to light color toward belly

SHORT-NOSED GAR
(Lepisosteus platostomus)

Beak 1/2 length of head

OTHER NAMES

Mississippi Alligator Gar, Billy Gar, Gar Pike, Billfish, Manjuari, Duckbill Gar, Gar Jack, Needle Nose Gar, Shortbill Gar

REPRODUCTION

Gars spawn during the early spring, scattering their eggs in weed beds. A mature female can lay between 47,000 and 77,000 eggs.

LARGEMOUTH BASS
(Micropterus salmoides)

The largemouth bass is the most popular and most sought-after game fish in North America. Its distribution covers lakes and rivers throughout Canada, Mexico, and the United States.

Largemouth bass can be caught bait casting, spinning, or fly fishing. Spring and fall are the best seasons to fish for largemouths, working shorelines, rock piles, and weed beds. In the summer months, fish water 12 to 15 feet deep, adjacent to weed beds or lily pads.

WORLD RECORD

RECORD HOLDER: George W. Perry
WEIGHT: 22 lbs., 4 oz.
LENGTH: 32-1/2"
GIRTH: 22-1/2"
CAUGHT: June 2, 1932
WHERE: Montgomery Lake, Georgia

BASS FACTS

The largemouth bass is most active when the water temperature is between 68° and 75° F.

■ ■ ■ ■

The northern variety reaches a weight of 10 pounds, while the southern variety can exceed 20 pounds.

■ ■ ■ ■

Largemouth bass prefer crayfish over any other type of natural live bait.

■ ■ ■ ■

The average life span of the largemouth bass is four to six years.

BEST LURES

Some of the best-proven bass lures are illustrated below. Every tackle box should have an assortment of these basic lures.

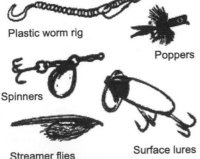

Plastic worm rig

Poppers

Spinners

Streamer flies

Surface lures

Diving lures

Spoons

Fish Identification

LIFE SPAN

The average bass lives four to six years, but the female bass lives longer and grows faster than the male.

GROWTH

Bass grow more in length during the first year of life than during the second year, but gain weight in the second and later years more than in the first year.

POUND FOR POUND

3 to 5 pounds of natural food

=

1 pound of bass

It takes 3 to 5 pounds of natural food to produce 1 pound of bass.

FEMALE

SUPER DAD

MALE

The male bass keeps vigil over the nest until the eggs hatch and protects the fry for about ten days, until they scatter.

OTHER NAMES

Bucketmouth, Big Mouth, Black Bass, Green Bass, Green Trout

REPRODUCTION

A good size, healthy female bass can lay up to 15,000 eggs.

MUSKELLUNGE
(Esox masquinongy)

The muskie is the largest member of the pike family and is known to exceed 80 pounds in weight. Its distribution covers Canada and the northern United States from New York to the Great Lakes.

It prefers shallow, weedy areas in lakes and rivers and will strike large plugs, spoons, spinners, or live baits such as suckers, chubs, or frogs. Casting large baits or lures around logs or weed beds will produce the best results.

WORLD RECORD

RECORD HOLDER: Art Lawton
CAUGHT: September 22, 1957
WHERE: St. Lawrence River, New York
WEIGHT: 69 lbs., 15 oz.
LENGTH: 64-1/2"
GIRTH: 31-3/4"

——— BEST LURES ———

Large surface
or diving lures

Large
spoons

Large buck tail
spinners

Fish Identification

LIFE SPAN AND SIZE

The average life span of the muskie is fifteen years and the average size is 30 inches. However, they can reach 6 feet in length and weigh as much as 100 pounds.

Most muskies caught are in the 10–15 pound range and come out of waters that are 10 feet deep or better.

MUSKELLUNGE
(Esox masquinongy)

IDENTIFICATION

The following illustrations show some of the distinguishing characteristics for identifying a muskie.

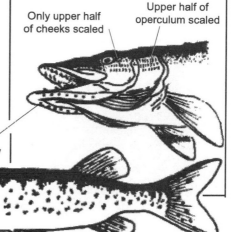

Only upper half of cheeks scaled

Upper half of operculum scaled

12 to 18 pores on underside of jaw

OTHER NAMES

Lunge, Great Pike, Blue Pike, Masquinongy

TIGER MUSKIE

Tiger muskies are a cross between a muskellunge and a northern pike and cannot reproduce.

TIGER MUSKIE
(Esox masquinongy immaculatus)

BEST BAITS

Perch

Suckers

Chubs

Frogs

REPRODUCTION

Reproductive age: three to four years
Spawning time: spring, eggs scattered
Number of eggs: 10,000 to 265,000
Days to hatch: twelve to fifteen

HABITAT

Prefers shallow water (10 feet deep) in and around weed beds, submerged logs, or brush piles.

NORTHERN PIKE
(Esox lucius)

Northern pike are abundant in most lakes and rivers in the northern parts of the United States and in Canada.

They prefer shallow weedy areas, grow to an average size of 32 inches, and weigh from 4 to 5 pounds. Larger fish of 10 to 15 pounds are common, with some reaching or exceeding 50 pounds.

The best time to fish for northerns is in the spring or fall, using natural baits such as live chubs, roaches, or artificial lures (spoons and spinners).

WORLD RECORD

RECORD HOLDER: Jiri Blaha
CAUGHT: December 9, 1979
WHERE: Lipno Reservoir, Czechoslovakia
WEIGHT: 55 lbs., 15-3/4 oz.

BEST LURES

Every pike fisherman's tackle box should have an assortment of the following lures.

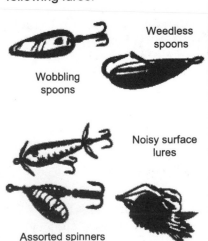

Wobbling spoons

Weedless spoons

Noisy surface lures

Assorted spinners

UNITED STATES RECORD

RECORD HOLDER: Peter Dubucin
CAUGHT: September 15, 1940
WHERE: Sacandaga Reservoir, New York
WEIGHT: 46 lbs., 2 oz.

Fish Identification

REPRODUCTION

The female northern reproduces after three years of age. Spawning time is early spring, in marshy areas, where the eggs are scattered in weed beds. A mature female can lay up to 2,000 eggs.

IDENTIFICATION

The illustration below shows some of the characteristics of a pike that can be used to distinguish it from other related species.

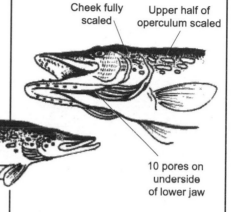

Cheek fully scaled

Upper half of operculum scaled

10 pores on underside of lower jaw

OTHER NAMES

Northern, Water Wolf, Snake, Jack, Hammer Handle

LIFE SPAN

The average life span of the northern pike is eight to ten years.

FEEDING HABITS

Pike grab bait fish crosswise when they strike, and then they turn the bait headfirst before swallowing.

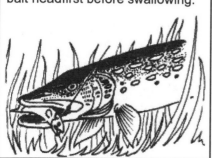

BEST BAITS

The most preferred baitfish of the pike are listed in order below.

1. Gizzard shad

2. Small carp

3. Fathead minnow

4. White sucker

PERCH
(Perca)

The perch is the little cousin of the walleye and sauger. It makes for excellent eating and is a favorite catch of most people who fish. Its distribution covers most fresh waters along the eastern Atlantic seaboard (south to the Carolinas), the Great Lakes region, and the Mississippi Valley.

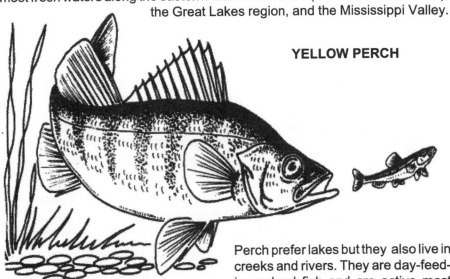

YELLOW PERCH

Perch prefer lakes but they also live in creeks and rivers. They are day-feeding school fish and are active most any time of the year.

Still or fly fishing using live bait or small flies and lures is very effective. Trolley line or power line fishing can also be used in the Great Lakes region.

BEST BAITS

A few of the more popular baits and lures to use for perch fishing are shown below.

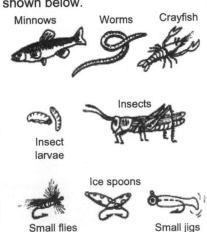

Minnows   Worms   Crayfish

Insect larvae   Insects

Ice spoons

Small flies   Small jigs

WORLD RECORD

RECORD HOLDER: Dr. C. C. Abbot
CAUGHT: May, 1865
WHERE: Bordentown, New Jersey
WEIGHT: 4 lbs., 3-1/2 oz.

PERCH FAMILY SUBDIVISIONS

DIVISION 1. Includes the walleye and sauger.

DIVISION 2. Includes the Eurasian and American yellow perch.

DIVISION 3. Includes the darters, of which there are about ninety species.

IDENTIFICATION

Two of the key characteristics distinguishing the walleye, the sauger, and the yellow perch are the eyes and mouth.

The eyes of the perch have pigmentation (color), while the eyes of the walleye and sauger do not. Also both the walleye and the sauger have distinct teeth, which the yellow perch lacks. In addition, the nose of the yellow perch can be used for identification to determine if your catch is really a perch or a darter, as shown below.

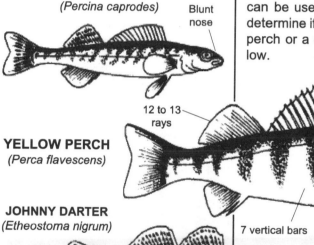

LOG PERCH
(Percina caprodes) Blunt nose

12 to 13 rays

YELLOW PERCH
(Perca flavescens)

JOHNNY DARTER
(Etheostoma nigrum)

Pigmentation in eyes

No teeth

7 vertical bars

Pelvic fins close together

Blunt nose

OTHER NAMES

Ringed Perch, Ringtail Perch, Lake Perch

LIFE SPAN

The average life span of the perch is seven to eight years, and it can reach a weight of 4 pounds, with the average weight being about 1/4 pound.

REPRODUCTION

Female perch reproduce after one year of age. An adult female can lay between 5,800 and 48,000 eggs. Spawning takes place in the spring, with the female laying her eggs in bands on weed beds to which the eggs adhere. The eggs hatch in twelve to twenty-one days, depending on the temperature of the water.

PICKEREL
(Esox niger)

The pickerel is common from Maine to Florida and throughout the Mississippi Valley. It prefers weedy lakes and quiet streams and is active all year long. It can be caught by bait casting, spinning, or fly fishing using an assortment of artificial lures such as wobbling spoons, spinners, or streamer flies. It can also be caught still fishing with live baits such as minnows, chubs, crayfish, and worms.

Early morning and dusk are the best times to fish for this little scrapper, in sheltered weedy bays or shallows with sunken logs and good weed cover.

WORLD RECORD
EASTERN CHAIN PICKEREL

RECORD HOLDER: B. McQuaig, Jr.
CAUGHT: February 17, 1961
WHERE: Homerville, Georgia
WEIGHT: 9 lbs., 6 oz.
LENGTH: 31"
GIRTH: 14"

BEST BAITS

Spoons   Minnows   Chubs

Spinners   Streamer flies   Worms   Crayfish

Fish Identification

The pickerel is the smallest member of the pike family, which includes the northern pike and the muskellunge. They are all very similar in shape with many common characteristics. They are voracious feeders and prey on smaller fish and minnows.

IDENTIFICATION

There are two species of pickerel found in the United States. Both are very similar in characteristics with the exception of size.

The grass pickerel seldom grows over 15 inches, while the chain pickerel can attain a length of 30 inches or more. Other distinguishing differences in the two species are indicated below.

Color is usually a dark black or brownish green shading to a greenish yellow, with the dark green markings connecting to form a chain pattern on the sides.

Cheeks and gill cover fully scaled

Dark "teardrop" markings

CHAIN PICKEREL
(Esox niger)

Color is usually dark green shading to a greenish yellow with brownish green bars along the sides. Lacks spots on sides or fins.

Cheeks and gill cover fully scaled

GRASS PICKEREL
(Esox americanus)

REPRODUCTION

Pickerel spawn in the early spring as soon as the ice melts, over shallow flooded areas or in the shallows of lakes and streams. They scatter their eggs along the weed beds, and the eggs hatch in twelve to fifteen days. The young grow very quickly and mature when they are two to four years old.

OTHER NAMES

Pickerel, Grass Pike, Jackfish, Mud Pickerel, Little Pickerel, Slough Pike, Redfin Pickerel, Banded Pickerel, Black Pike, Green Pike

ROCK BASS

(Ambloplites rupestris)

The rock bass with its big ruby red eyes, is a favorite among those who fish pan-fish. It prefers rocky or gravel bottoms It prefers rocky or gravel bottoms in lakes and rivers throughout the eastern United States and the upper Mississippi Valley.

Another member of the sunfish family also called a rock bass is the warmouth bass *(Lepomis gulosus)*. They both take any bait used in bluegill fishing and bite during most of the day. Natural baits such as grubs, worms, insects, and minnows produce the best results. In addition, small artificials such as wet flies, poppers, spinners, and jigs are very effective.

Fly or still fishing near rock piles, piers, or sunken logs produces the best results.

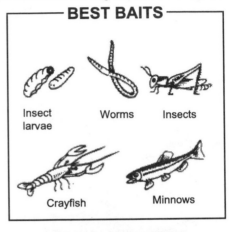

BEST BAITS

Insect larvae

Worms

Insects

Crayfish

Minnows

WORLD RECORDS
ROCK BASS
RECORD HOLDER: Peter Gulgin
CAUGHT: August 1, 1974
WHERE: York River, Ontario
WEIGHT: 3 lbs., 0 oz.
LENGTH: 13-1/2"
GIRTH: 10-3/4"

WARMOUTH BASS
RECORD HOLDER: Tony D. Dempsey
CAUGHT: October 19,1985
WHERE: Yellow River, Florida
WEIGHT: 2 lbs., 7 oz.

Fish Identification

LIFE SPAN AND SIZE

The life span of a rock bass is about four years, reaching an average size of 6 or 7 inches in length.

ROCK BASS
(Ambloplites rupestris)

IDENTIFICATION

The following illustration points out identifying characteristics for both types of sunfish known as rock bass. Both species have the same basic shape, but they vary in coloration and other characteristics.

Brassy color with rows of darker spots on scales

Red eye

Medium mouth

6 anal spines

WARMOUTH BASS
(Lepomis gulosus)

Brassy color with mottled dark brown

Dark bars radiating from eyes

3 anal spines

Large mouth with teeth on tongue

REPRODUCTION

A female matures between one and two years of age and spawns in the late spring (May through June). Rock bass build nests by scooping out depressions in gravel or sand beds. They lay between 2,000 and 11,000 eggs. The eggs hatch in five to ten days.

OTHER NAMES

Goggle-eye, Red Eye Bass, Rock Sunfish, Red Eye, Mud Bass, Weed Bass, Wood Bass

SALMON
(Salmonidae)

In North America, salmon range from the pacific coast of California to Alaska and along the upper east coast from New York to Canada.

They spend most of their adult lives in salt water, but they enter freshwater rivers and streams during their spawning migrations, at which time they lay their eggs and die.

They are also found in the Great Lakes region, where they were introduced through stocking programs by various conservation groups. These salmon spend their entire lives in fresh water. Salmon can be caught by bait casting, trolling, or fly fishing, using an assortment of baits, lures, and flies.

WORLD RECORDS

COHO SALMON
RECORD HOLDER: Mrs. Lee Hallberg
CAUGHT: October 11, 1947
WHERE: Cowichan Bay,
British Columbia
WEIGHT: 31 lbs.

CHINOOK SALMON
RECORD HOLDER: Heinz Wichmann
CAUGHT: July 19, 1959
WHERE: Skeena River,
British Columbia
WEIGHT: 92 lbs.
LENGTH: 58-1/2"
GIRTH: 36"

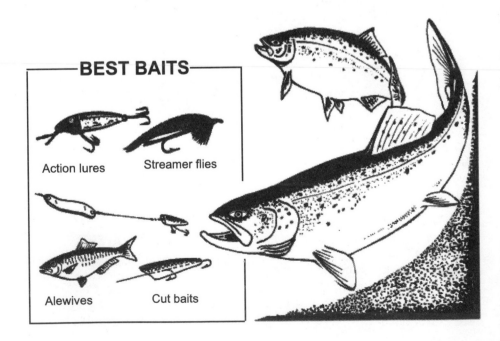

BEST BAITS

Action lures

Streamer flies

Alewives

Cut baits

Fish Identification

SALMON FAMILY

The salmon family *(Salmonidae)* includes the trouts, charrs, whitefishes, sheefish, and the ciscoes as well as the salmons.

── IDENTIFICATION ──

Because of the large number of species in the salmon family, only the two most common species are illustrated below.

Black spots on upper lobe of tail

Black spots on back

COHO SALMON
(Oncorhynchus kisutch)

12 to 15 rays

Black spots on both lobes of tail

Black spots on back and dorsal fin

Teeth of lower jaw in grayish gum

14 to 17 rays

Teeth of lower jaw in black gums

CHINOOK SALMON
(Oncorhynchus tschawytscha)

REPRODUCTION

All salmon spawn in fresh water and eventually migrate to salt water (except for the Great Lakes or landlocked salmon) until they mature and reach reproductive age at three to five years. They then return to the streams or rivers where they were hatched or introduced, to spawn and die.

Adult female salmon lay between 3,000 and 4,000 eggs, which hatch in sixty to ninety days.

OTHER NAMES

CHINOOK SALMON:
King Salmon, Tyee, Spring Salmon

COHO SALMON:
Silver Salmon, Hoopid Salmon, Kisutch Salmon

SMALLMOUTH BASS
(Micropterus dolomieui)

The smallmouth bass, one of the largest members of the sunfish family, can be found in lakes and rivers from Canada to the southern United States (except the Gulf States).

It likes clear, cool waters with rocky, stone, or gravel bottoms.

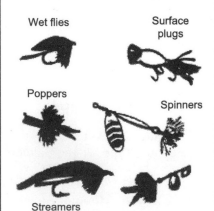

It is most active in the late spring and the fall months and is a day and night feeder.

Fly and spin fishing are the best methods to use, with spinners, flies, plugs or buck tails producing the best results.

─── BEST LURES ───
These lures and flies are just a few of those recommended for smallmouth bass fishing.

Wet flies

Surface plugs

Poppers

Spinners

Streamers

WORLD RECORD

RECORD HOLDER: David L. Hayes
CAUGHT: July 9, 1955
WHERE: Dale Hollow Lake, Kentucky
WEIGHT: 11 lbs., 15 oz.
LENGTH: 27"
GIRTH: 21-2/3"

─── BEST BAITS ───

Minnows

Insects

Crayfish

Worms

Fish Identification

Described here are just a few facts relating to the smallmouth bass.

LIFE SPAN AND SIZE

The average life span is five to six years, and the average size is about 1/2 pound.

IDENTIFICATION

Because of its close resemblance to the largemouth bass, the following characteristics of the smallmouth should be considered for a positive identification.

Dark stripes in vertical bars along the sides

13 to 15 rays

11 scale rows

Upper jaw does not extend beyond eye

Jaw extends beyond eye

SMALLMOUTH BASS
(Micropterus dolomieui)

LARGEMOUTH BASS
(Micropterus salmoides)

HABITAT

The smallmouth bass is less tolerant of poor water quality than the largemouth bass.

REPRODUCTION

The smallmouth bass spawns in the spring and is a nest builder, laying eggs that hatch in three to six days. The female reaches reproductive age at two years and can lay as many as 2,000 to 21,000 eggs.

OTHER NAMES

Smallmouth Black Bass, Bronzeback, Redeye

STRIPED BASS
(Roccus)

The striped bass family consists of the white and yellow bass and a hybrid relative of the saltwater striped bass.They are found in many of the rivers, large lakes, and impoundments throughout the United States. Striped bass are deep water fish, and are usually caught by fishing areas with sandy or gravel bottoms. Trolling live baits and artificial lures or still fishing deep water are the most effective methods to use.

WORLD RECORD

WHITE BASS

RECORD HOLDER: P.S. Cordell
CAUGHT: March 31, 1977
WHERE: Longhorn Dam, Texas
WEIGHT: 5 lbs., 9 oz.

YELLOW BASS

RECORD HOLDER: D. Stalker
CAUGHT: March 27, 1977
WHERE: Monroe County, Indiana
WEIGHT: 21 lbs., 4 oz.

HYBRID STRIPED BASS

RECORD HOLDER: F. Smith
CAUGHT: May 26, 1977
WHERE: Colorado River, Arizona
WEIGHT: 59 lbs., 12 oz.

—BEST BAITS—

Spoons

Shad

Spinners

Streamers

HYBRID STRIPED BASS

Fish Identification

The freshwater striped bass (hybrid) is actually a landlocked cousin of the saltwater species. It is stocked in many lakes and reservoirs throughout the United States.

The yellow and white bass are both freshwater relatives of the hybrid species and are found in lakes and rivers throughout the Mississippi drainage area.

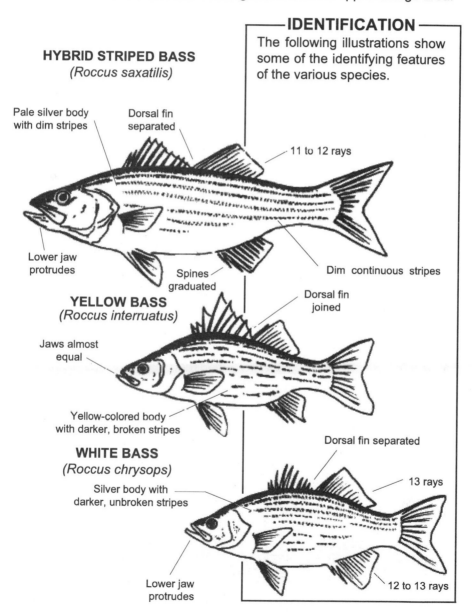

── IDENTIFICATION ──

The following illustrations show some of the identifying features of the various species.

HYBRID STRIPED BASS
(Roccus saxatilis)

Pale silver body with dim stripes

Dorsal fin separated

11 to 12 rays

Lower jaw protrudes

Spines graduated

Dim continuous stripes

YELLOW BASS
(Roccus interruatus)

Jaws almost equal

Dorsal fin joined

Yellow-colored body with darker, broken stripes

WHITE BASS
(Roccus chrysops)

Silver body with darker, unbroken stripes

Dorsal fin separated

13 rays

Lower jaw protrudes

12 to 13 rays

SUNFISH
(Lepomis)

Sunfishes make up the largest family of freshwater game fish in North America. There are twenty-five different species of sunfish, which include the bass and the bluegill family, and they can be found in most lakes, ponds, rivers, and streams throughout the United States. Sunfish prefer clear, clean waters with weedy cover and a sandy or gravel bottom. They are active all year long, with insects and snails as their principal foods.

Fly and still fishing in and around weed beds are the best methods to use when fishing for sunfish.

■■■■

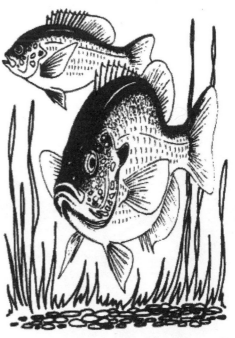

─── BEST BAITS ───

Some of the more popular baits and lures to use for sunfish are shown below.

Maggots   Grubs   Leaf worms

Crickets   Grasshoppers

Small flies   Ice spoons   Small jigs

WORLD RECORDS

(Due to the large number of species in the sunfish family, only the records for the green and the redear sunfish are listed below.)

GREEN SUNFISH
RECORD HOLDER: Paul Dilly
CAUGHT: June 18, 1971
WHERE: Stockton Lake, Missouri
WEIGHT: 2 lbs., 2 oz.
LENGTH: 14-3/4"
GIRTH: 14"

REDEAR SUNFISH
RECORD HOLDER: Maurice E. Ball
CAUGHT: June 19, 1970
WHERE: Chase City, Virginia
WEIGHT: 4 lbs., 8 oz.
LENGTH: 16-1/4"
GIRTH: 17-3/4"

Fish Identification

LIFE SPAN

The average life span of the sunfish is four to six years, and the average size is 1/4 pound, or 3 to 4 inches in length.

IDENTIFICATION

Because of the large number of species in the sunfish family, identification of specific family members can be somewhat difficult. However, one of the key characteristics to look for on all sunfish is the anal fin. All sunfish have at least three strong spines on the anal fin. Other distinct characteristics are coloration and the ear on the gill cover behind the eye.

REDEAR SUNFISH
(Lepomis macrolophus)

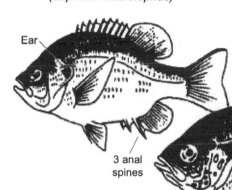

Ear

3 anal spines

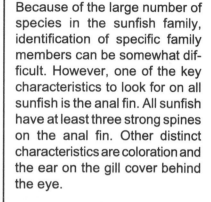

Yellow edges

GREEN SUNFISH
(Lepomis cyanellus)

REPRODUCTION

Sunfish reach reproductive age after one or two years. They are nest builders and spawn from May through August. A mature female can lay from 2,000 to 10,000 eggs, depending on the species, and the eggs hatch in five to ten days. After the eggs hatch, the male sunfish guards the young fry in the nest until they are large enough to scatter.

OTHER NAMES

Shellcrackers, Stumpknockers, Red Breasts, Perch, Creek Perch, Black Perch, Longears

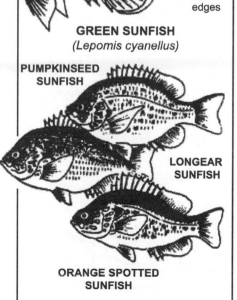

PUMPKINSEED SUNFISH

LONGEAR SUNFISH

ORANGE SPOTTED SUNFISH

TROUT
(Salmo)

Trout are widespread throughout the world. They are found in the colder streams, rivers, and lakes of many countries. The trout family consists of a large number of species and subspecies that vary in color, body form, and other characteristics.

WORLD RECORDS

RAINBOW TROUT

RECORD HOLDER: D.R. White
CAUGHT: May 22, 1970
WHERE: Bell Island, Alaska
WEIGHT: 42 lbs., 2 oz.
LENGTH: 43"
GIRTH: 23-1/2"

BROWN TROUT

RECORD HOLDER: W. Muir
CAUGHT: 1886
WHERE: Loch Awe, Scotland
WEIGHT: 39 lbs., 8 oz.

BEST BAITS

A trout's principal food consists of insects and insect larvae, which makes fly fishing one of the most effective methods to use when pursuing these hardy scrappers.

Dry flies, wet flies, and streamers, as well as natural baits such as insects or insect larvae, are very productive.

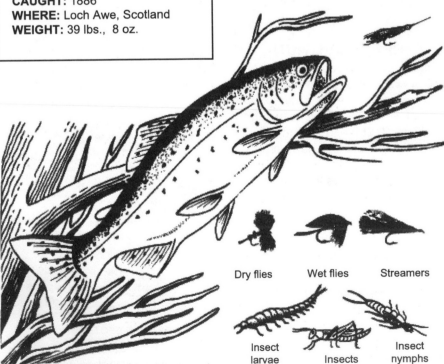

Dry flies   Wet flies   Streamers

Insect larvae   Insects   Insect nymphs

Fish Identification

TROUT FAMILY

Most trout are found in the northern parts of the world (north of latitude 40). They are divided into two groups—the salmo group and the charr group *(Salvelinus)*.

IDENTIFICATION

Salmo group: Includes rainbows, goldens and the cutthroats.
Charr group: Includes brooks, lakes, arctic sunapees, and the dolly vardens.

Only three of the many species in the trout family are illustrated below.

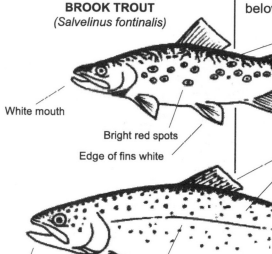

BROOK TROUT
(Salvelinus fontinalis)

White mouth

Bright red spots

Edge of fins white

Worm-like markings

Tail nearly square with irregular markings

10 to 12 rays

White mouth

Pink line

Spots on dorsal fin, back, and tail

9 to 12 rays

RAINBOW TROUT
(Oncorhynchus gairdneri)

Yellow to orange spots with halos

No markings on tail

10 to 12 rays

BROWN TROUT
(Salmo trutta)

OTHER NAMES

BROOK TROUT: Speckled Trout, Charr, Brookie
RAINBOW TROUT: Steelhead
BROWN TROUT: German, Brownie, Loch Leven

REPRODUCTION

Most species spawn from early spring to early summer except the members of the charr group, which spawn in the autumn.

WALLEYED PIKE
(Stizostedion vitreum)

The walleye is not a true member of the pike family, but a member of the perch family, related to the sauger, the darters, and the yellow perch. Its distribution covers Europe, Asia, Canada, and the United States.

It is basically a night feeder and is most active in the spring and fall. In the daytime, walleyes are usually in deeper water over rocks or sunken brush piles.

Walleyes are school fish, so if you catch one, you are apt to find others in the same place.

Fish for walleyes by deep trolling, using spinners, jigs, or live baits. After locating a school, anchor and work the area for the best results.

BEST BAITS

Some of the most productive live baits and lures used for walleyes are shown below.

LIVE BAITS

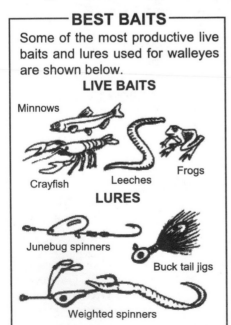

Minnows

Crayfish   Leeches   Frogs

LURES

Junebug spinners

Buck tail jigs

Weighted spinners

BEST RIG

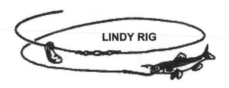

LINDY RIG

WORLD RECORD

RECORD HOLDER: Mabry Harper
CAUGHT: August 1, 1960
WHERE: Old Hickory Lake, Tennessee
WEIGHT: 25 lbs.
LENGTH: 41"
GIRTH: 29"

FISHING BASICS

LIFE SPAN AND SIZE

The life span of the walleye can be as long as ten to twelve years. The average size of a mature walleye is 1 to 4 pounds.

IDENTIFICATION

The walleye has a smaller relative with similar characteristics called the sauger. Because of its similarity to the sauger, the following characteristics should be considered for a positive identification.

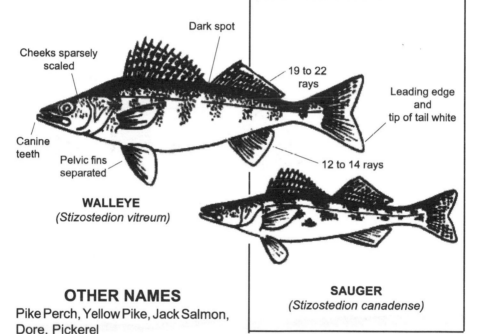

Dark spot

Cheeks sparsely scaled

19 to 22 rays

Leading edge and tip of tail white

Canine teeth

Pelvic fins separated

12 to 14 rays

WALLEYE
(Stizostedion vitreum)

SAUGER
(Stizostedion canadense)

OTHER NAMES

Pike Perch, Yellow Pike, Jack Salmon, Dore, Pickerel

REPRODUCTION

The female walleye starts to reproduce at three years of age. The average female can lay between 35,000 and 65,000 eggs. Spawning time is early spring in shallow water, where the female scatters her eggs along the bottom.

HABITAT

Except during spawning, the walleye prefers deep water with a rocky bottom that has cover such as brush piles.

PRINCIPAL FOOD

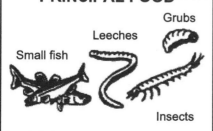

Grubs

Leeches

Small fish

Insects

MINNOWS

The following illustration shows the most common minnows used as live bait and the characteristics that identify them.

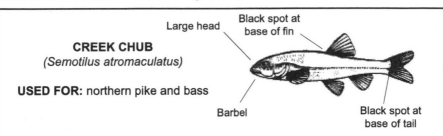

CREEK CHUB
(Semotilus atromaculatus)

USED FOR: northern pike and bass

Large head

Black spot at base of fin

Barbel

Black spot at base of tail

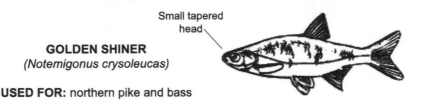

GOLDEN SHINER
(Notemigonus crysoleucas)

USED FOR: northern pike and bass

Small tapered head

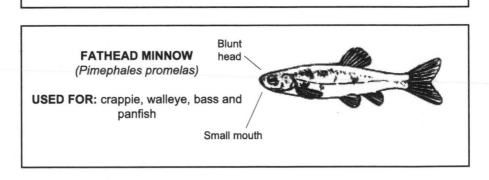

FATHEAD MINNOW
(Pimephales promelas)

USED FOR: crappie, walleye, bass and panfish

Blunt head

Small mouth

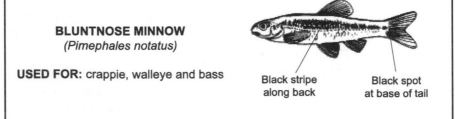

BLUNTNOSE MINNOW
(Pimephales notatus)

USED FOR: crappie, walleye and bass

Black stripe along back

Black spot at base of tail

Chapter 10

LURE MAKING

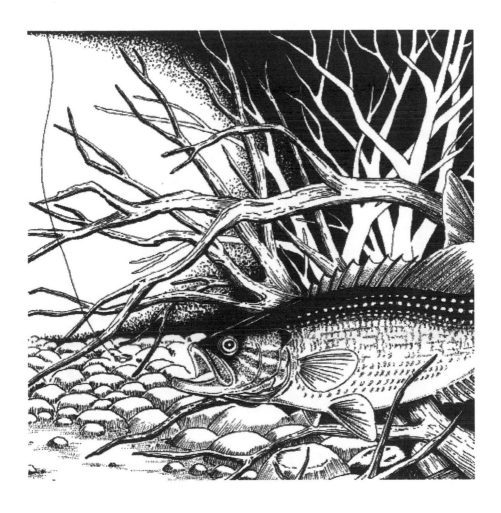

BASIC TOOLS AND MATERIALS

The illustrations below and on the next page show some of the basic tools and materials required to make your own lures (including plugs, spinners, jigs, spoons, and buzzbaits). You can purchase most of them at your local tackle shop or through any of the many mail order houses that deal in fishing equipment. The type of tools and materials you will be using will vary depending on the type of lure you are trying to make.

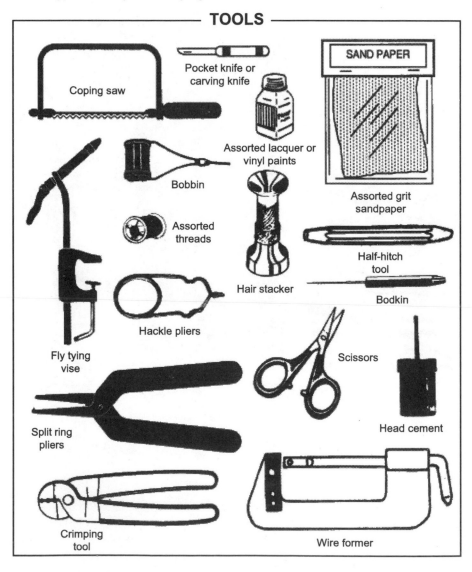

— **TOOLS** —

Coping saw

Pocket knife or carving knife

SAND PAPER

Assorted lacquer or vinyl paints

Bobbin

Assorted threads

Assorted grit sandpaper

Half-hitch tool

Hair stacker

Bodkin

Hackle pliers

Fly tying vise

Scissors

Split ring pliers

Head cement

Crimping tool

Wire former

Lure Making

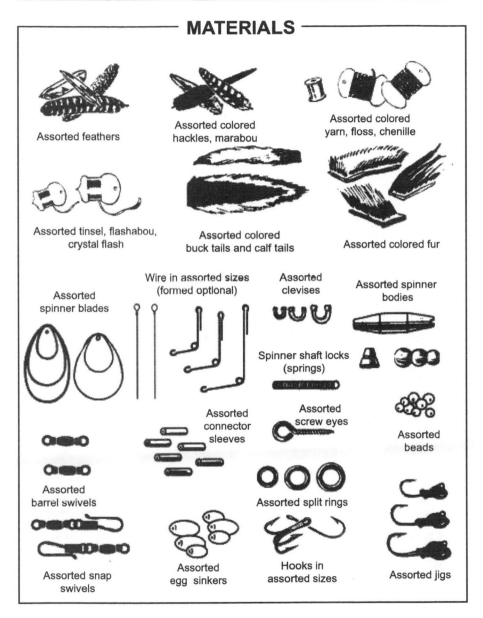

The following pages contain the basic instructions for making lures and other types of fishing gear (for example, leaders and slip sinkers). Each type of lure can be varied depending on the materials you use and how creative you want to be.

MAKING PLUGS

You can make a variety of plugs, either from store-bought material (already shaped plastic bodies) or by carving your own from a block of wood.

The following illustrations show the materials, tools, and components required to make your own plugs. Most of the tools can be found in the average home, and the materials or components can be purchased at most tackle shops or from a mail order tackle dealer.

MATERIALS

Selecting the material for the plug you want to build is important.

Most wooden plugs are made of basswood or red cedar. Both of these woods have a smooth grain finish and are easy to carve. You can purchase wood blocks in assorted sizes through most mail order tackle dealers or you can get the wood at your local lumber yard.

COMPONENTS

Components such as hooks, plastic-formed bodies, screws, and hook eyes, shown below, must be purchased from your local tackle shop or mail order tackle dealer.

REQUIRED TOOLS

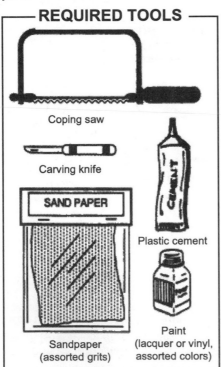

Coping saw

Carving knife

SAND PAPER

Plastic cement

Sandpaper
(assorted grits)

Paint
(lacquer or vinyl,
assorted colors)

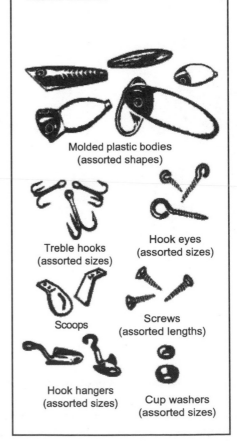

Molded plastic bodies
(assorted shapes)

Treble hooks
(assorted sizes)

Hook eyes
(assorted sizes)

Scoops

Screws
(assorted lengths)

Hook hangers
(assorted sizes)

Cup washers
(assorted sizes)

PLASTIC PLUG ASSEMBLY

STEP 1

Most purchased plastic plug bodies come as two pieces, either a front and a back or a left and right side. Regardless of their type, they must be glued together using plastic plug cement and allowed to dry.

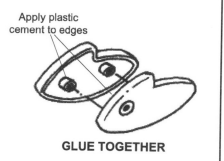

Apply plastic cement to edges

GLUE TOGETHER

STEP 2

After the plug is glued together, remove any burrs or excess cement with a piece of fine grit sandpaper.

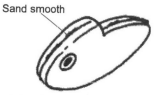

Sand smooth

REMOVE BURRS/SAND SMOOTH

STEP 3

Paint the plug the desired colors using vinyl paints (three coats) and again allow it to dry.

Lacquer or vinyl paint

3 coats

PAINT BODY THREE COATS

STEP 4

After the plug is completely dry, you can attach the hook eyes or hook hangers, hooks, scoop, and line eye to the plug, using a small screwdriver.

Your plug is now complete and ready to use.

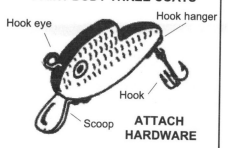

Hook eye

Hook hanger

Hook

Scoop

ATTACH HARDWARE

WOODEN PLUGS: CARVING AND ASSEMBLY

The next two pages give examples of the steps necessary to make a wooden plug. The examples shown are for a panfish plug and a crankbait. The same method used in the construction of both these plugs can be applied to make a wooden equivalent of any of the premolded plugs available today. All it takes is the time and a minimal investment in the tools and components.

PANFISH PLUGS

MATERIALS
■ One block of basswood or cedar, 1/4" thick x 3/4" wide x 1-1/4" long
■ One soda or beer can tab
■ Two hook eyes
■ One treble hook
■ Epoxy cement (glue)
■ Light green, black, and white model paint

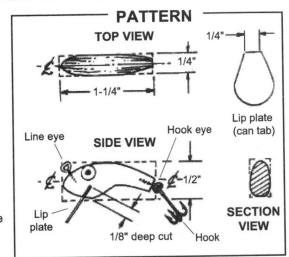

PATTERN

TOP VIEW

1/4"
1/4"
1-1/4"

Lip plate (can tab)

Line eye   **SIDE VIEW**   Hook eye

1/2"

Lip plate

1/8" deep cut   Hook

SECTION VIEW

INSTRUCTIONS

STEP 1
Trace the pattern onto the wood block.

Pattern

Wood block

STEP 2
Cut out the pattern with a coping saw.

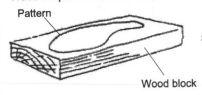

Allow pattern to show

STEP 3
Shape the body with a razor or knife to the proper dimensions and sand smooth with #120 grade sandpaper.

Shape and sand smooth

STEP 4
Cut a slot for the lip plate with a coping saw per the dimensions below and glue the plate into position.

Slot

1/4" deep

Glue

Glue lip plate (can tab) into position

STEP 5
Paint the plug body as shown (three coats) and paint in the eyes. After the paint dries, attach the line eye, hook eye, and hook.

Top of body dark green

Outer rim white

Inner rim black

Body sides silver

Underside white

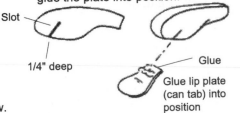

CRANKBAITS

PATTERN

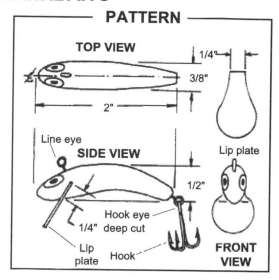

TOP VIEW

1/4"

3/8"

2"

Line eye

SIDE VIEW

Lip plate

Hook eye

1/4" deep cut

1/2"

Lip plate   Hook

FRONT VIEW

MATERIALS

- One block of basswood or red cedar, 3/8" thick x 1/2" wide x 2" long
- One soda or beer can tab
- Two hook eyes
- One treble hook
- Epoxy cement (glue)
- Light green, black, and white model paint

INSTRUCTIONS

STEP 1
Trace the pattern onto the wood block.

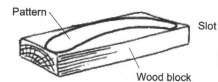

Pattern

Slot

Wood block

STEP 2
Cut out the pattern with a coping saw.

Allow pattern to show

STEP 3
Shape the body with a razor or knife to the proper dimensions and sand smooth with #120 grade sandpaper.

Shape and sand smooth

STEP 4
Cut a slot for the lip plate with a coping saw per the dimensions below and glue the plate into position.

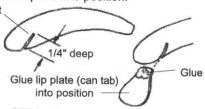

Slot

1/4" deep

Glue

Glue lip plate (can tab) into position

STEP 5
Paint the plug body as shown (three coats) and paint in the eyes. After the paint dries, attach the line eye, hook eye, and hook.

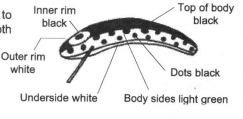

Inner rim black

Top of body black

Outer rim white

Underside white

Body sides light green

Dots black

HOW TO DRESS JIGS

To get started in dressing your own jigs, you will need the following tools and materials.

TOOLS

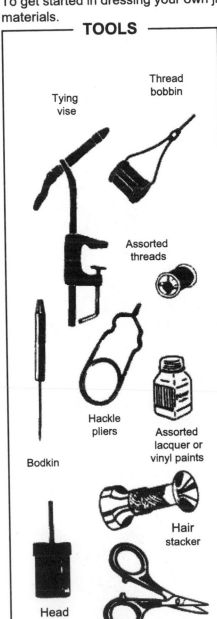

Tying vise

Thread bobbin

Assorted threads

Hackle pliers

Bodkin

Assorted lacquer or vinyl paints

Hair stacker

Head cement

Scissors

MATERIALS

The first requirement in materials for dressing jigs is the jighead itself. You can cast your own if you buy a jig mold, jig hooks, and the lead, or you can purchase pre-cast jigheads at most tackle shops. Many tackle shops carry a vast variety of pre-cast jigs in different sizes, shapes, and colors that are reasonably priced and will eliminate a lot of work involved in casting or painting your own.

The second material requirement is to have an assortment of feathers, furs, and tinsels in a variety of colors. Most of these items can be obtained as individual items or in a jig tying kit, which can also be purchased at most sporting goods stores. The advantage of buying a kit is that it also includes the equipment or tools, such as a vise, bobbin, and hackle pliers, for dressing jigs.

ASSORTED JIGHEADS, FEATHERS, FURS AND TINSELS

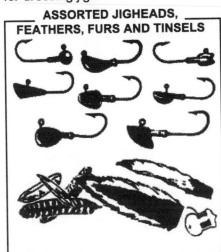

DRESSING

STEP 1
Paint the jighead the desired color and allow it to dry. After it is dry, secure the jighead in the vise as shown below.

STEP 2
If you are going to have a feather or tinsel tail, lay down a base of thread along the hook shank from the head to the bend of the hook.

STEP 3
Tie in the tail material on top of the thread base and tie off with a half-hitch.

STEP 4
Lay down a thread base along the jighead collar.

STEP 5
Tie in your choice of material (such as feathers or fur) around the collar, as shown below, and secure it with a half-hitch.

STEP 6
Select a long saddle hackle, strip part of the stem, and tie it in just behind the jighead.

STEP 7
Using your hackle pliers, wrap (palmer) the hackle around the collar (three or four wraps) and secure it with your thread.

STEP 8
Finish off with a couple of half-hitches, tie off (cut the thread), and coat the thread with head cement. Your jig is now complete.

SPOONS

Here's a way to cut down on the costs of buying those expensive ready-made lures. All you need are a few household tools, a few barrel swivels, split rings, and hooks, which can be purchased at a tackle shop for a few pennies, and some old silverware spoons you can pick up at a neighborhood garage sale or flea market.

SILVERWARE SPOONS

STEP 1
Remove the handle from a teaspoon or tablespoon using a hacksaw. Then grind or file the cut end smooth.

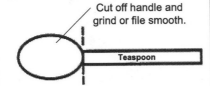

Cut off handle and grind or file smooth.

Teaspoon

STEP 2
Drill a small hole at each end of the spoon as shown below.

Drill hole

Drill hole

STEP 3
Attach the swivel, split rings, and hook as shown below.

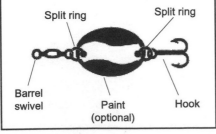

Split ring

Split ring

Barrel swivel

Paint (optional)

Hook

SPINNER BLADE SPOONS

Another type of spoon that's easy to make is the spinner blade spoon. All you need are some spinner blades in assorted sizes and styles, which you can purchase at most tackle shops. Then drill another hole at the blade end and attach the swivel, split rings, and hook the same way you did for the silverware spoon.

BLADE STYLES

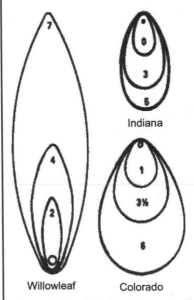

7

4

2

Willowleaf

0
3
5
Indiana

0
1
3½
6
Colorado

For additional flash, put some adhesive-backed prismatic sheet material on the blade.

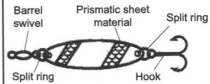

Barrel swivel

Prismatic sheet material

Split ring

Split ring

Hook

SPOON-MAKING TIP

When making spoons using either silverware or spinner blades, try different-shaped blades or styles.

Each shape has its own action. Some shapes will flutter back and forth and others will wobble.

──FLY ROD SPOONS──

By using small spinner blades, split rings, and your favorite wet fly or streamer, you can make an effective light spoon for fly casting.

STEP 1
Drill two small holes, one at each end of the spinner blade.

Drill hole

Drill hole

STEP 2
Attach a small split ring through each hole at both ends.

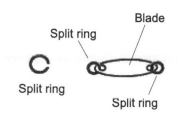

Blade

Split ring

Split ring

Split ring

STEP 3
Attach your favorite wet fly or streamer to one of the split rings, as shown below.

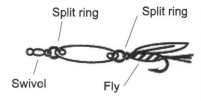

Split ring

Split ring

Swivel

Fly

── ICE SPOONS ──

Here's another type of spoon you can make with a spinner blade. You can use it for ice fishing or fly casting.

STEP 1
Starting with a small spinner blade (sizes 00, 0 or 1), solder a small hook to the inner side of the blade, as shown below.

TOP VIEW

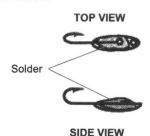

Solder

SIDE VIEW

STEP 2
File the soldered surface smooth and paint the entire blade the color of your choice.

TOP VIEW

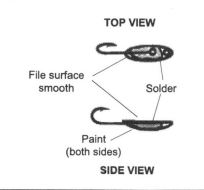

File surface smooth

Solder

Paint
(both sides)

SIDE VIEW

SPINNERS

When making a spinner, it is important to remember a few factors as follows.

In most spinner designs, the weight or body should be behind the blade rather than in front of it. If you want the weight or body in front of the blade, it should be fixed to the shaft so it won't slide down and stop the blade from spinning. Keep this in mind when you start your spinner assembly.

To start making spinners, one of the best investments is a wire former. This tool will allow you to form the shafts and all of the bends (eyes, loops, safety pin snap bends) that are required in a spinner construction.

WIRE FORMER TOOL

The wire former shown below is only one of many types available today.

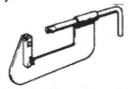

The following illustrations show a few of the many bends that can be made with a wire former.

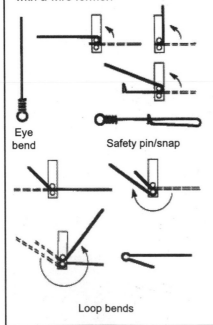

Eye bend

Safety pin/snap

Loop bends

NAIL METHOD FOR BENDS AND LOOPS

If you don't have a wire forming tool, here's an alternative way to make the bends and loops on purchased shafts that have a wrapped eye, which will require additional bending.

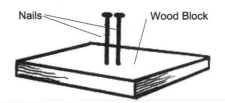

Nails — Wood Block

Just pound a couple of nails into a wooden block far enough apart to slip the wire between them. Make the bends as shown below.

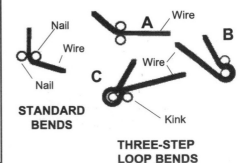

Nail

Wire

Wire

A Wire

B

C

Wire

Nail

Kink

STANDARD BENDS

THREE-STEP LOOP BENDS

SPINNER COMPONENTS AND ASSEMBLY

To make your own spinners you will need certain components, which are illustrated below.

With the exception of the wire shafts, which can be formed with a wire former, you can purchase the majority of the components from your local tackle shop or through a mail order tackle supply catalog at a reasonable price.

COMPONENTS

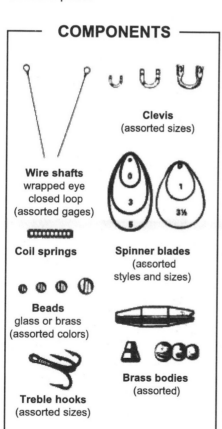

Wire shafts
wrapped eye
closed loop
(assorted gages)

Coil springs

Beads
glass or brass
(assorted colors)

Treble hooks
(assorted sizes)

Clevis
(assorted sizes)

Spinner blades
(assorted
styles and sizes)

Brass bodies
(assorted)

ASSEMBLY

STEP 1
Starting with the wire shaft, slip on the components in the following order.

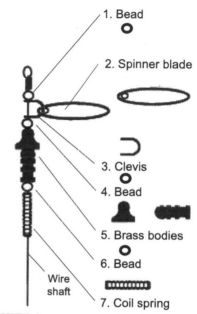

1. Bead

2. Spinner blade

3. Clevis

4. Bead

5. Brass bodies

6. Bead

Wire shaft

7. Coil spring

STEP 2
After all the components are on the shaft, make an open loop bend on the unbent part of the shaft using the wire former or a pair of pliers, as shown below.

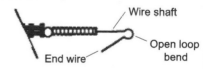

Wire shaft

Open loop bend

End wire

STEP 3
After the bend is made, trim the end wire so that the coil spring can be pulled down, as shown below.

Coil spring over wire

Add hook

BUZZBAITS

Buzzbaits are a common lure used for fishing bass as well as other species. The lure is fished by using a fast retrieve, causing the blade to churn the water surface, which creates a commotion that attracts fish.

The items shown below are the tools and components required to make a buzzbait. You can make the body of the lure by using a wire former and attaching a jig, as shown in the instructions, or you can use purchased pre-formed bodies for the assembly. You can also cast your own body forms with the jig in place by using a buzzbait mold.

The pre-formed bodies or the buzzbait mold, as well as the delta blades shown below, can be purchased from most tackle shops or mail order tackle supply houses.

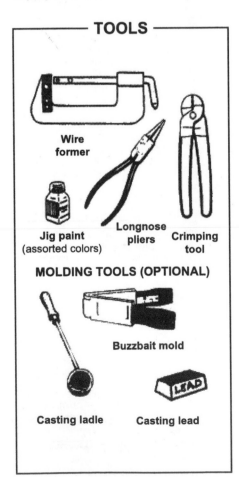

TOOLS

Wire former

Jig paint
(assorted colors)

Longnose pliers

Crimping tool

MOLDING TOOLS (OPTIONAL)

Buzzbait mold

Casting ladle

Casting lead

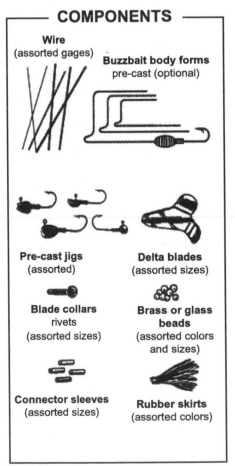

COMPONENTS

Wire
(assorted gages)

Buzzbait body forms
pre-cast (optional)

Pre-cast jigs
(assorted)

Delta blades
(assorted sizes)

Blade collars
rivets
(assorted sizes)

Brass or glass beads
(assorted colors and sizes)

Connector sleeves
(assorted sizes)

Rubber skirts
(assorted colors)

── WIRE BODY CONSTRUCTION ──

The following instructions for forming the basic wire for a buzzbait apply only if you choose to make your own form.

Starting with a 12-inch piece of wire (.028 or .035 diameter), form the wire to the proportions shown at right.

Note: *The larger or heavier the jighead, the larger diameter wire.*

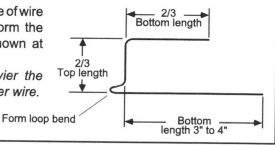

── ASSEMBLY ──

STEP 1
Begin by painting the jighead, whether it is a pre-formed casted wire with the head attached or a loose jighead. Next, slip the blade collar (narrow end first) or a bead onto the top wire, as shown in the illustration below.

STEP 2
Slip the delta blade or tandem blades onto the top wire, as shown below, followed by several beads. After the components are in place, bend the end of the wire slightly with your longnose pliers. With the pre-formed casted wire, your buzzbait is now complete. If you formed your own wire, go to the next step.

STEP 3
Slip a connector sleeve (proper diameter for wire gage being used) onto the bottom wire, followed by the loose jighead, and form a loop bend in the bottom wire approximately where the top wire ends. Move the jighead back to the loop and slip the open end of the bottom wire into the connector sleeve, crimping the sleeve with your crimping tool. Finish off your buzzbait by slipping on a rubber skirt.

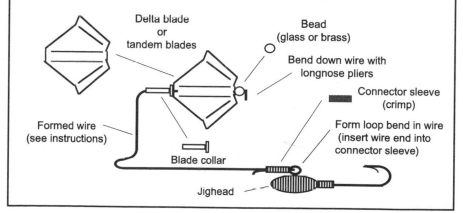

SPINNER BAITS

Spinner baits are popular lures for bass, northerns, muskies, and other game fish. The lure is fished by using a fast retrieve causing the blade to vibrate and spin in the water, which creates a commotion that attracts fish.

The items shown below are the tools and components required to make a spinner bait. You can make the body of the lure by using a wire former and attaching a jig, as shown in the instructions, or you can cast the body with the jighead in place by using a spinner bait mold. You can purchase the lure body form (pre-cast jighead in place) from most tackle shops or mail order tackle supply houses if you choose not to form or cast your own.

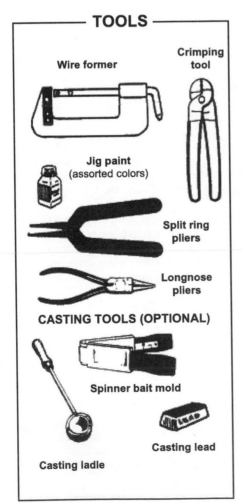

— TOOLS —

Wire former

Crimping tool

Jig paint (assorted colors)

Split ring pliers

Longnose pliers

CASTING TOOLS (OPTIONAL)

Spinner bait mold

Casting lead

Casting ladle

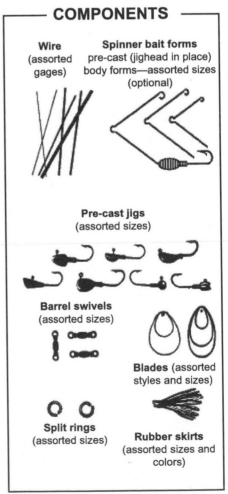

— COMPONENTS —

Wire (assorted gages)

Spinner bait forms pre-cast (jighead in place) body forms—assorted sizes (optional)

Pre-cast jigs (assorted sizes)

Barrel swivels (assorted sizes)

Blades (assorted styles and sizes)

Split rings (assorted sizes)

Rubber skirts (assorted sizes and colors)

WIRE BODY CONSTRUCTION

The following instructions for forming the basic wire for a spinner bait apply only if you choose to make your own form rather than purchasing pre-formed/cast spinner bait forms.

Starting with a 12-inch piece of wire (.028 or .035 diameter), form the wire to the proportions shown.

Note: *The larger or heavier the jighead, the larger diameter wire.*

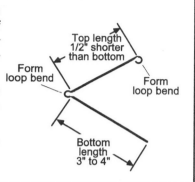

ASSEMBLY

STEP 1
First, paint the jighead, whether it is a pre-formed casted wire with the head attached or a loose jighead. Next, attach the proper size barrel swivel, split ring, and spinner blade to the top wire and close the loop bend with your longnose pliers. With the pre-formed casted wire form, your spinner bait is now complete, except for adding the rubber skirt. If you formed your own wire, go to the next step.

STEP 2
Slip a connector sleeve (proper diameter for wire gage being used) onto the bottom wire, followed by the loose jighead, and form a loop bend in the bottom wire. Move the jighead back to the loop, slip the open end of the bottom wire into the connector sleeve, and crimp the sleeve with your crimping tool. Finish off your spinner bait by slipping on a rubber skirt.

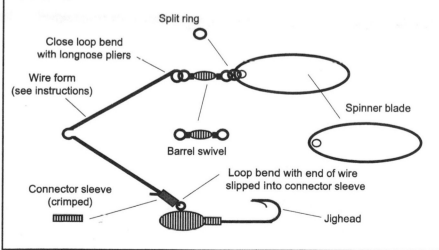

SPINNER, SPINNER BAIT, AND BUZZBAIT VARIATIONS

You may want to try the following variations in the designs and assemblies of spinners, spinner baits, and buzzbaits.

┌─ SPINNER VARIATIONS ─┐

Rather than attaching a plain treble hook to the end of your spinner, try some of the fly patterns shown below.

┌─ BUZZBAIT VARIATIONS ─┐

Change the bends, wire lengths, and the assembly, as shown below, to design your own buzzbait creation.

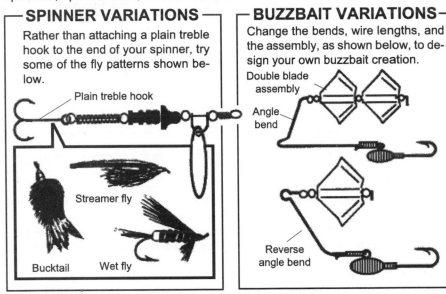

── SPINNER BAIT VARIATIONS ──

A change in bends, types of blades you use, jigheads, and so forth allows for a multitude of spinner bait designs. All you need is a little imagination.

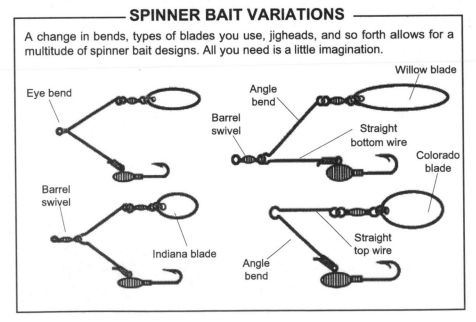

Lure Making

MINNOW HARNESS

Here's a simple harness you can make for trolling minnows when you're out walleye fishing. All you need are a few tools, spinner components, and a double hook, which you can purchase at your local tackle shop.

COMPONENTS

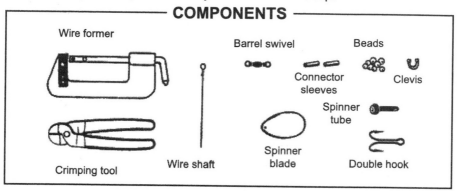

Wire former

Barrel swivel

Beads

Connector sleeves

Clevis

Spinner tube

Crimping tool

Wire shaft

Spinner blade

Double hook

ASSEMBLY

STEP 1

Starting with a 12" piece of wire, form a loop at one end of the wire using the wire former.

STEP 2

Slip the barrel swivel and a connector sleeve onto the wire. Slide the swivel into the loop and the end of the wire into the connector sleeve, and crimp it with your crimping tool.

STEP 3

Slip a couple of beads onto the wire shaft, followed by the clevis (with the spinner blade through the clevis), followed by a couple of more beads, followed by the spinner tube and another connector sleeve.

STEP 4

After all the components are in place, form another loop at the opposite end of the shaft, slip the wire end into the connector sleeve, and crimp it with your crimping tool. Attach the double hook to the shaft after the bait is put on the harness, as shown below.

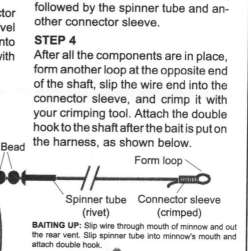

Spinner blade

Barrel swivel

Clevis

Bead

Form loop

Spinner tube (rivet)

Connector sleeve (crimped)

Form loop

Bead

Connector sleeve (crimped)

BAITING UP: Slip wire through mouth of minnow and out the rear vent. Slip spinner tube into minnow's mouth and attach double hook.

Slip into mouth

Vent opening

Double hook

WORM HARNESS

Fishing with a worm harness is a common practice used around Lake Erie and in the Midwest. The following instructions describe a simple harness that you can make, using a few tools and spinner components that you can purchase at your local tackle shop.

COMPONENTS

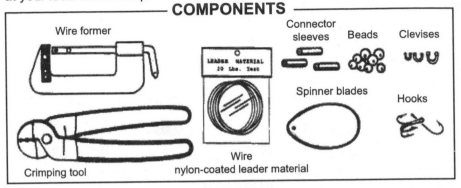

ASSEMBLY

STEP 1
Starting with a 20" piece of leader material, slip on a connector sleeve and a treble hook. Form a loop around the hook eye by slipping the end of the leader material back into the connector sleeve and then crimping the sleeve with the crimping tool.

STEP 2
From the opposite end of the leader material, slip on another connector sleeve, followed by a hook (#8 through #12). Form another loop around the hook eye as you did in step 1 with the connector sleeve. Position the hook approximetly 2" away from the treble hook, snug up the loop, and crimp the sleeve.

STEP 3
Repeat step 2 with another hook 2" away from the last hook.

STEP 4
Slip on a couple of beads, followed by a clevis (with a spinner blade through the clevis), followed by two more beads, followed by another connector sleeve. After all the components are in place, make a loop at the end of the leader material, bring back the last connector sleeve, insert the loose end of the loop into the sleeve, and crimp it with your crimping tool. Your worm harness is now complete.

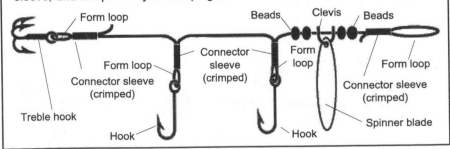

SLIP SINKER RIGS

Here's a way to save a few dollars by making your own slip sinker rigs. All you need are a few tools and components, which you can purchase at any tackle shop at a reasonable cost. The assembly takes only a little time.

── TOOLS AND COMPONENTS ──

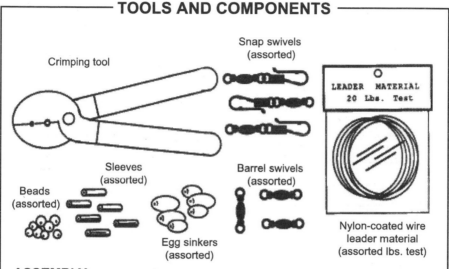

Crimping tool

Snap swivels (assorted)

LEADER MATERIAL
20 Lbs. Test

Beads (assorted)

Sleeves (assorted)

Barrel swivels (assorted)

Egg sinkers (assorted)

Nylon-coated wire leader material (assorted lbs. test)

ASSEMBLY:

Starting with a 15" piece of leader material, slip on a sleeve and a barrel swivel at one end, and then form a loop with the material, bringing the end back and through the sleeve. Crimp the sleeve with the crimping tool. Next slip on a bead, egg sinker, another bead, and another sleeve, and crimp the second sleeve 4" below the first one you put on. Next, slip on a third sleeve and a swivel snap, and bring the remaining end back through the sleeve, forming another loop. Crimp the third sleeve, and your slip sinker rig is complete.

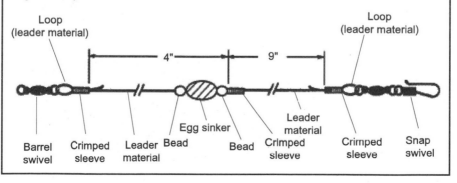

Loop (leader material)

Loop (leader material)

4"   9"

Barrel swivel | Crimped sleeve | Leader material | Bead | Egg sinker | Bead | Leader material | Crimped sleeve | Crimped sleeve | Snap swivel

CASTING LEADERS

You can also save a few dollars by making your own casting leaders. All you need are a few tools and a few components, which you can purchase at your local tackle shop, and a little spare time for the assembly.

TOOLS AND COMPONENTS

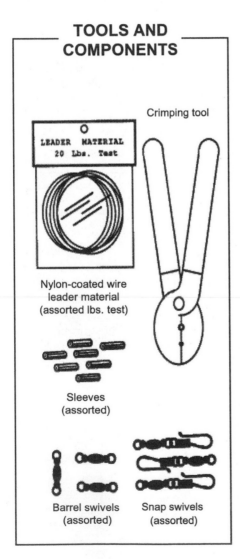

Crimping tool

LEADER MATERIAL
20 lbs. Test

Nylon-coated wire
leader material
(assorted lbs. test)

Sleeves
(assorted)

Barrel swivels
(assorted)

Snap swivels
(assorted)

— ASSEMBLY —

Starting at one end of a piece of leader material (length of your choice), slip on a sleeve and a barrel swivel. Form a loop with the end, slip it back through the sleeve, and crimp it with the crimping tool. At the opposite end, slip on another sleeve and a snap swivel, and do the same thing (crimp).

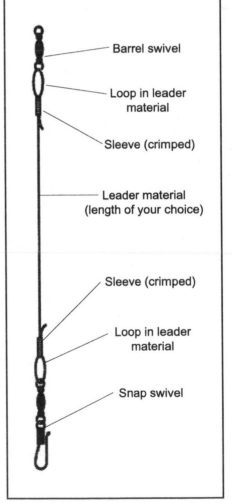

Barrel swivel

Loop in leader material

Sleeve (crimped)

Leader material (length of your choice)

Sleeve (crimped)

Loop in leader material

Snap swivel

Chapter 11

FLY TYING

BASIC TOOLS

To get started in fly tying, you will need some basic tools, which in most cases you will be able to purchase at your local tackle shop or through a fishing tackle mail order house.

For the beginner, the best approach to getting started is to purchase a fly tying kit. Most kits will include all of the basic tools as well as a selection of assorted materials that are used to tie various types of patterns. The kits vary in price from $20.00 or less to over $100.00, depending on what you choose.

Once you learn the basics using a kit and you wish to improve your skills, you'll be ready to purchase better equipment.

The illustration below shows the various tools required in fly tying. In addition, the following pages contain information on how to make some of your own tools, such as the bodkin, half-hitch tool, hair stacker, dubbing twister, and bobbin.

BASIC FLY TYING TOOLS

Hackle pliers

Threader

Bodkin

Tying vise

Thread bobbins

Assorted threads

Hair stacker

Scissors

Head cement

HOMEMADE TOOLS

Many of the tools used in fly tying can be made at home and will work as well as those purchased in a kit or from a manufacturer.

The following illustrations show how to make your own bodkins, half-hitch tools, hair stackers, dubbing twisters and bobbins. All you need are a few items that you can purchase from a craft store or hobby shop, some old discards you may have in your home, and a few household tools to use for assembly.

—— HOMEMADE BODKIN ——

Here's a way to reuse those old, dried-up ballpoint pens that we throw away after they won't write anymore.

STEP 1

Remove the inner workings from both the top and bottom parts of an old ballpoint pen so that only the shell or case remains.

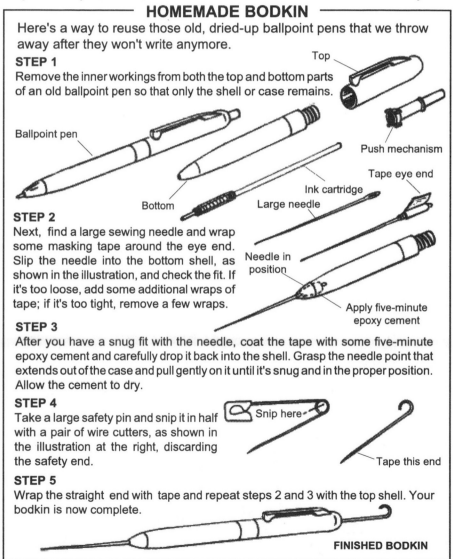

STEP 2

Next, find a large sewing needle and wrap some masking tape around the eye end. Slip the needle into the bottom shell, as shown in the illustration, and check the fit. If it's too loose, add some additional wraps of tape; if it's too tight, remove a few wraps.

STEP 3

After you have a snug fit with the needle, coat the tape with some five-minute epoxy cement and carefully drop it back into the shell. Grasp the needle point that extends out of the case and pull gently on it until it's snug and in the proper position. Allow the cement to dry.

STEP 4

Take a large safety pin and snip it in half with a pair of wire cutters, as shown in the illustration at the right, discarding the safety end.

STEP 5

Wrap the straight end with tape and repeat steps 2 and 3 with the top shell. Your bodkin is now complete.

FINISHED BODKIN

HALF-HITCH TOOL/HAIR COMPACTOR

Here's a simple tool you can make from a discarded felt tip marker. All that you need to do is to remove the felt from the marker and clean out the case.

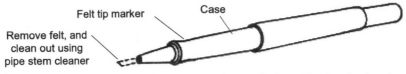

Felt tip marker   Case

Remove felt, and clean out using pipe stem cleaner

You can also use this tool to compact spun hair on the hook shank when tying hair patterns. The following illustrations show how it works.

HALF-HITCH TOOL   **HAIR COMPACTOR**

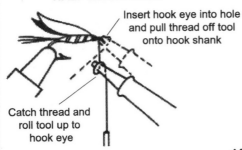

Insert hook eye into hole and pull thread off tool onto hook shank

Catch thread and roll tool up to hook eye

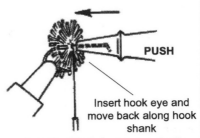

PUSH

Insert hook eye and move back along hook shank

Place the tool along the thread and give it a twist with your wrist, forming a loop around the end. Next, insert the hook eye into the end of the tool and pull the thread off of the tool.

After a bunch of hair is spun onto the hook shank, slip the hook eye into the tool and push the hair back along the shank, using the tool. Repeat the process for each bunch of hair you add to the hook shank.

HAIR STACKER
CIGAR TUBE

The next time you (or a friend) purchase an expensive cigar that comes in an aluminum tube, keep the tube—they make excellent hair stackers.

BERING
MILD CIGAR - TAMPA FLORIDA

Insert hair, cover, and tap cover on table surface

ALUMINUM CASE

Tips of hair face out, ends go into tube first

Fly Tying

DUBBING TWISTER

Here's an easy-to-make tool that's great to use with the loop method to apply dubbing to a hook.

STEP 1
Form a piece of wire purchased from a hobby or craft shop (.018 diameter thick and 12" long) to the shape shown in the following illustration, using a pair of longnose pliers.

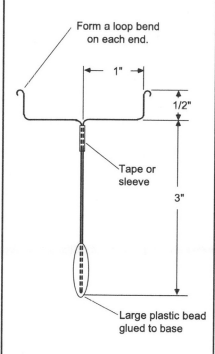

Form a loop bend on each end.

1"

1/2"

Tape or sleeve

3"

Large plastic bead glued to base

STEP 2
After you form the wire, tape or slip a small sleeve into the position shown in the illustration above. Then slip the end wires into a large plastic bead and secure with epoxy cement.

HOW IT WORKS

Hook the dubbing loop you formed with your thread into the loop bends of the twister tool. After the loop is dubbed, spin or twist the twister tool with your fingers to form a dubbed noodle. Wrap the hook shank with the noodle using your twister tool.

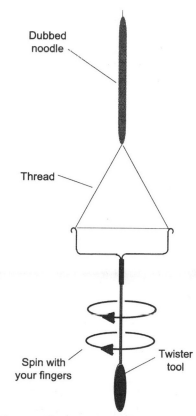

Dubbed noodle

Thread

Spin with your fingers

Twister tool

After you finish, secure the dubbed area with your thread, remove the twister tool from the remaining noodle, and snip off the excess noodle material.

THREAD BOBBIN

Here's a way to make inexpensive bobbins using a wire coat hanger and a few items that you can purchase at a hobby shop or a craft store.

STEP 1

Using a pair of wire cutters or your pliers, snip out the straight portion of a wire hanger, as shown in the illustration.

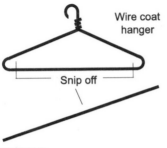

Wire coat hanger

Snip off

REQUIRED MATERIALS

■ One brass or aluminum tube, 2" long x 1/16" in diameter.
Note:Tubing can be purchased in 3-foot lengths from a craft or hobby shop and cut to desired lengths.
■ Two wooden beads, 7/16" in diameter.
Note: Beads can also be purchased in packages of twelve or more from a craft or hobby shop.
■ One wire coat hanger
■ One five-minute epoxy cement kit
■ As required: furnace or duct tape
■ Sandpaper, extra fine grit

STEP 2

Form the wire piece to the dimensions shown in the following illustration, using a pair of longnose pliers.

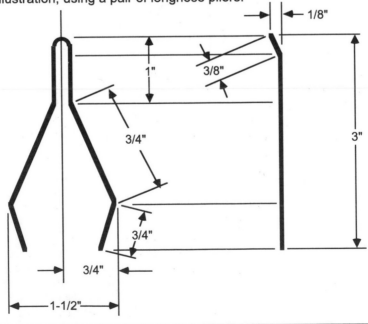

ASSEMBLY

STEP 3

Take the purchased brass or aluminum tubing and cut off a piece that's 2"
long. Sand both ends of the piece with fine grit sandpaper, removing any
burrs or sharp edges from both the outer and inner edges of the tube.
*Note: If you have some fine grade steel wool, use it to go over the sanded
areas. You can also check for burrs by using a cotton swab. Insert the swab
into the tube and pull back; if it snags, you'll need to do a little more sanding.*

Remove burrs and
sharp edges on both ends
(inside and outside)

Brass or
aluminun tube

2"- long section

STEP 4

Position the tube on the wire, as shown in the illustration, and glue it in place
with some epoxy cement. After the cement dries, wrap some duct tape
around the wire and tube as shown below.

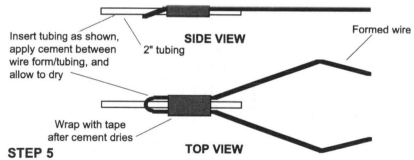

Insert tubing as shown,
apply cement between
wire form/tubing, and
allow to dry

SIDE VIEW

2" tubing

Formed wire

Wrap with tape
after cement dries

TOP VIEW

STEP 5

The final step in the bobbin assembly is to cement the wooden beads into
position. Apply some cement to the wire ends and to the inside of the holes
in the beads. Slip the beads onto the wire, as shown, and allow the cement
to dry. Your homemade bobbin is now ready to use.

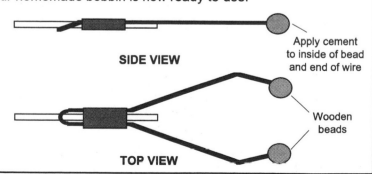

SIDE VIEW

Apply cement
to inside of bead
and end of wire

Wooden
beads

TOP VIEW

BASIC MATERIALS

One of the most frequently asked questions from a beginning fly tyer is "What kinds of materials will I need and where will I get them?"

The following illustration shows some of the various materials used in fly tying. You will find many of them in a fly tying kit, along with the basic tools, if you purchase a kit to get started. You can also purchase an assortment of materials from various sources such as fly tying catalog houses, craft shops, and sporting goods stores. Another source of fly tying materials can be from friends who hunt. In most cases, your friends will be glad to save you the feathers or fur from the game animals they've shot.

The following pages offer some tips on purchasing, storing, and selecting some of the more commonly used materials. Once you get started, you'll be amazed at the great variety of materials used in fly tying.

─── MATERIALS ───

Various patterns call for an assortment of materials. The following illustrations show some of the basic materials that you should have available when fly tying.

Assorted colors
of buck tails and calf tails

Assorted colored
hackles, marabou

Ostrich plumes in
assorted colors

Assorted fur
(rabbit, fox, squirrel,
deer, bear)

Assorted quills

Peacock
(herl, eye tail feathers,
sword feather)

Assorted
necks and saddles

Assorted
breast and flank
feathers

Assorted colors
of yarn,
floss, chenille

Assorted colors of
tinsel, flashabou,
crystal flash

MATERIAL TIPS
PURCHASING IMPORTED NECKS

One of the more frequently purchased items in fly tying is a neck (cape) from a game cock or rooster. The feathers found on the neck are used primarily to construct the wings and collars found on most dry flies. Below are a few tips to remember when purchasing imported necks.

IMPORTED NECKS (CAPES)

Many supply houses offer imported necks from China, India, or the Philippines. When purchasing imported necks, you can identify their origin by the shape of the skin patch at the back of the neck. A few characteristics of the patch to look for when trying to determine the neck's origin are:

■ **Chinese necks** have a bulb-shaped patch with a wide neck area.
■ **Philippine necks** are very similar to Chinese necks, except that the neck area is very narrow.
■ **Indian necks** have a square or rectangular-shaped patch, which makes their identification easiest.

The following illustration shows the different shapes of the skin patches found on the various necks.

QUALITY RANKING

BEST: Chinese necks are the best quality, with soft narrow stems, and thin, thoroughly scraped skins.
GOOD: Indian necks are of good quality, with thicker skin.
FAIR: Philippine necks are of fair quality, with larger and sometimes twisted hackles.

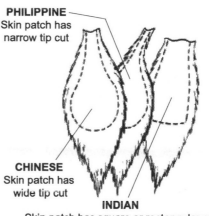

PHILIPPINE
Skin patch has narrow tip cut

CHINESE
Skin patch has wide tip cut

INDIAN
Skin patch has square or rectangular cut

STORING MATERIALS

Materials such as necks, bird skins, or buck tails should be kept in unsealed Ziploc® bags containing mothballs. If the bags are sealed, the natural oils contained in the skins will migrate to the feathers or hairs of the material.

Other materials such as plumage, strung hackles, tanned animal skins, calf tails, and squirrel tails should be kept in sealed Ziploc® bags or closed plastic boxes containing mothballs. Store your materials in a well-lit area; moths and other insects do the most damage in dark areas.

GAME COCK (Rooster) FEATHERS

The most commonly used feathers in fly tying come from the domesticated game cock or rooster. These birds are raised specifically for their feathers, which are used extensively in fly tying. The following illustrations show various feather locations on a game cock, their names, a brief description of each type of feather, and the type of pattern in which they are used.

NECK HACKLE (Cape):
Stiff-quilled narrow feathers that cover the neck and back of a rooster's head. Used for both dry and wet flies, as well as for streamers.

SPADE HACKLE:
Short, wide hackles found on the back and shoulder. Used for bass flies and streamers.

SADDLE HACKLE (Saddle Patch):
Long, thin feathers with flexible stems, found on the back between the spade hackles and the tail. Used for drys, wets, bass flies, streamers, and saltwater patterns.

SPEY HACKLE:
Short, wide hackles found near the base of the tail. Used for bass flies.

TAIL (COQUE) FEATHERS:
Long feathers located at the rump. Used for saltwater streamer patterns.

BODY FEATHERS (Body Patch):
Short, wide feathers located on the sides and belly. Used for wings or beards on drys, wets, bass bugs, streamers, and nymph patterns.

FEATHER NAMES AND LOCATIONS

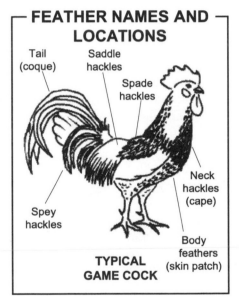

TYPICAL GAME COCK

FEATHERS

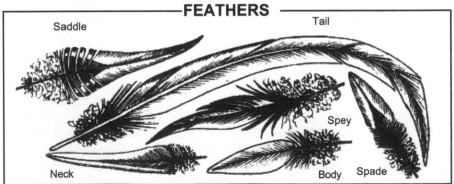

HACKLE SELECTION

The following illustration shows the average number of feathers found on a typical neck and the location of feathers to be used for a specific size hook. This general rule of thumb can vary depending on the size of each neck.

┌─ LOCATION AND SIZE ─┐

The following chart can be used as a quick reference for hackle selection, based on the hook size being used and the type of pattern being tied.

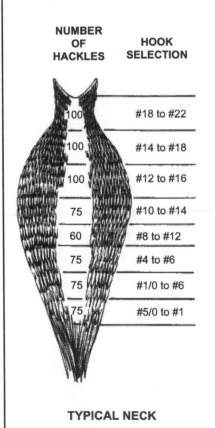

NUMBER OF HACKLES	HOOK SELECTION
100	#18 to #22
100	#14 to #18
100	#12 to #16
75	#10 to #14
60	#8 to #12
75	#4 to #6
75	#1/0 to #6
75	#5/0 to #1

TYPICAL NECK

┌─ HACKLE QUALITY ─┐

When selecting a hackle for a dry fly, wet fly, or streamer pattern, the amount of webbing in the feather selected must be considered. The following illustration shows what to look for when you make your selection.

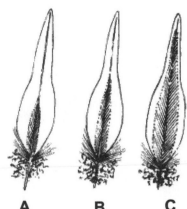

A	B	C
Minimum webbing	Medium webbing	Heavy webbing

A. Dry fly quality: Has the least amount of webbing.

B. Dry or wet fly quality: Has medium amount of webbing; also can be used for streamers.

C. Wet fly quality: Has heavy webbing; can also be used for streamer wings and collars, nymph hackles, and the like.

TYING BASICS

The following pages contain information on the basic techniques used to attach various types of materials to a hook. Also included are instructions for the two principal knots used in fly tying.

Learning how to make the knots and mastering the techniques will simplify and improve your tying ability as well as the quality of your finished fly patterns.

To become a good tyer, you need to practice, and to try different types of patterns that include the various methods used to attach the materials to the hook. The old saying "Practice makes perfect" is especially true when it comes to fly tying. The more you practice the better the results.

You might also want to get involved with a tying club, where you can witness the various techniques being applied by an accomplished tier. To find a local fly tying club in your area, write to The Federation of Fly Fishers, P.O. Box 1088, West Yellowstone, MT 59758. The Federation, a national organization that promotes fly fishing and fly tying, will be more than happy to assist you in finding a local club.

Fly tying is a relaxing and satisfying hobby, and it is extremely gratifying to catch fish on a fly that you tied or a pattern you created. Fly tying will provide you with many hours of fun and enjoyment, and it's not very difficult to learn.

Give it a try!

BASIC KNOTS

─── HALF-HITCH ───

STEP 1
Catch the thread with two fingers.

STEP 2
Form a loop by flipping your hand over and opening your fingers.

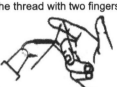

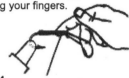

STEP 3
Bring the thread to the hook shank and slip the eye of the hook into the open loop.

STEP 4
Place your index finger on the shank over the thread and pull the thread tight with your bobbin.

─── WHIP FINISH ───

STEP 1
Catch the thread with two fingers.

STEP 2
Form a loop by flipping your hand over.

STEP 3
Bring the thread to the hook shank and open the loop by spreading your fingers.

STEP 4
Pass the loop to the back, over the hook shank (shank into open loop), and close your fingers.

STEP 5
Rotate the loop from the back forward and repeat steps 4 and 5 three or four times.

STEP 6
Stop the loop at the top of the hook and pull the thread tightly with your bobbin, releasing the loop as you pull.

HOOK AND THREAD ATTACHMENT

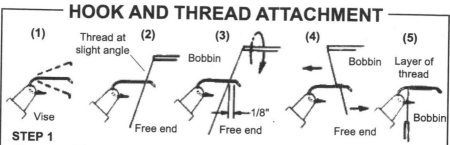

(1) Vise

(2) Thread at slight angle, Bobbin, Free end

(3) Free end, 1/8"

(4) Bobbin, Free end

(5) Layer of thread, Bobbin

STEP 1
Always level the hook in the vise and hide as much of the point and barb as possible.

STEP 2
Hold the free end of the thread with one hand and the bobbin with your other hand, and place the thread against the hook shank at a slight angle.

STEP 3
Start the thread about 1/8" behind the hook eye and make a half-turn around the shank while maintaining tension with both hands.

STEP 4
Continue wrapping the thread with the bobbin to the rear, while moving the free end forward to the eye, causing the thread to wrap over itself.

STEP 5
After you've made about six wraps, snip off the excess or free end and continue to wrap until you have a layer of thread just short of the bend of the hook.

TYING IN TAILS

Various patterns call for many different materials to be used as tails, but they are all attached in the following fashion.

(1)

(2)

STEP 1
Select the material for the tail, place it between your fingers, and lay it firmly at the back of the hook on top of the shank. Also, grab the shank with your fingers to keep the material from turning and to keep it in position. Hold this position until the entire sequence of wraps is completed.

STEP 2
Make three wraps over the material toward the back and one wrap under the material. Bring the thread forward and make an additional three wraps over the top of the material, going forward. Make a half-hitch and snip off the excess material at the front.

MATERIAL VARIATIONS

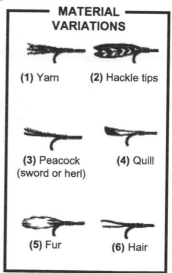

(1) Yarn

(2) Hackle tips

(3) Peacock (sword or herl)

(4) Quill

(5) Fur

(6) Hair

TYING IN BODIES

Various patterns call for many different materials to be used when tying in a body. Some patterns call for two or three different materials in the body construction. Nevertheless, they are all attached to the hook in the same basic manner. A basic body construction found on most streamer or wet fly patterns is shown below.

BODY CONSTRUCTION

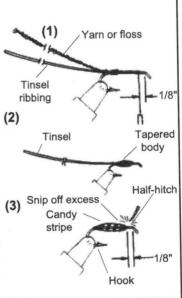

STEP 1
After laying down a thread base, tie in the base material (yarn or floss) for the body at the back of the hook. Next, tie in the ribbing (tinsel, for example) at the same spot and snip off the excess. Then bring the thread forward to within 1/8" of the hook eye.

STEP 2
Form a tapered body with the yarn or floss material by wrapping forward and then back until the body is cigar-shaped. Secure the material with your thread and snip off the excess.

STEP 3
Starting at the back, give the tinsel a single wrap at the back of the hook. Then wrap the tinsel forward over the yarn or floss, creating a candy stripe effect and keeping the spaces equal. Secure the tinsel behind the eye with a half-hitch, and snip off the excess.

BODY VARIATIONS

EGG SAC (Butt)

Tie in a strand of peacock herl at the back of the hook. Make four to six wraps with the herl (one on top of the other) and secure it with your thread.

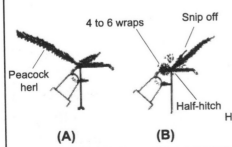

(A)   **(B)**

PALMERED HACKLE

Tie in a piece of yarn or floss and a hackle feather at the back of the hook. Form the body with the yarn or floss and secure it with your thread. Next, wrap the hackle over the body, forward to the hook eye. Snip off the excess and secure with a half-hitch.

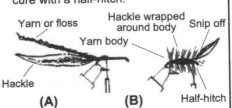

(A)   **(B)**

DUBBING

Dubbing consists of furs or various materials cut and blended together to form a matting to be used for body construction. Most dubbing is applied to the thread with a twisting motion, which creates a furry strand that is then wrapped around the shank of the hook. The following illustrations show a few ways to apply the dubbing to the thread.

CONVENTIONAL METHOD

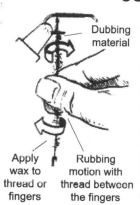

Dubbing material

Apply wax to thread or fingers

Rubbing motion with thread between the fingers

STEP 1
Start by applying a small amount of soft dubbing wax to your thread or fingers. Then, apply sparse amounts of dubbing material to the thread, using a rubbing motion of the fingers with the thread between them.

STEP 2
After you apply 3" to 4" of dubbing to the thread, start wrapping your body with the dubbed thread until you need more material. Then repeat step 1 as often as required until the body is completed.

Form body by wrapping dubbed thread around hook shank

3" to 4" of dubbed thread

DUBBING LOOP METHOD

STEP 1
Starting at the back of the hook, form a loop with your thread. Secure the loop at the back with your thread, and then bring the thread forward to the front of the hook.

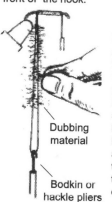

Dubbing material

Bodkin or hackle pliers

Noodle

Thread loop

Twist loop

STEP 2
Apply tension to the bottom of the loop by hooking it with your bodkin or hackle pliers. Then apply the dubbing material to the loop by sandwiching the material between the loop threads. Be sure to use sparse amounts of dubbing material and spread the material evenly on both sides of the thread.

STEP 3
After the material is between the loop, start twisting (spinning) the thread loop with your bodkin or hackle plier until you form a noodle with the thread loop.

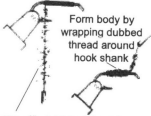

STEP 4
Form the body with the noodle going foward and secure it with your thread. Snip off the excess part of the noodle.

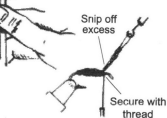

Snip off excess

Secure with thread

SPINNING HAIR

The following illustrations show the basic steps used to spin hair onto a hook shank.

——— INSTRUCTIONS ———

STEP 1

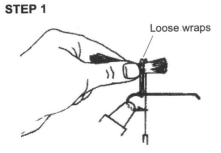

Loose wraps

Starting with a clump of hair that you can hold comfortably between your fingers, put a couple of loose wraps about a third of the way up the length of the hair at the back of the hook shank.

Note: Use a strong thread like Monocord or size "E."

STEP 2

Bring the clump of hair down on the shank of the hook and tighten the loose wraps by pulling down with your bobbin.

STEP 3

Tighten up loose wraps by pulling down.

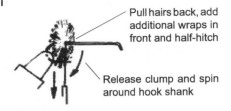

Pull hairs back, add additional wraps in front and half-hitch

Release clump and spin around hook shank

When the wraps start to tighten, release the clump and continue to add a few additional wraps through the clump as it turns around the hook shank. With your free hand, pull back the hairs at the front of the clump, and add some additional wraps and a half-hitch.

STEP 4

Put a drop of head cement over the half-hitch and at the front of the clump.

STEP 5

Add drop of cement to half-hitch and clump of hair

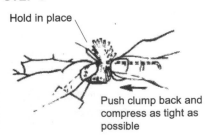

Hold in place

Push clump back and compress as tight as possible

Repeat steps 1 through 4 for each clump of hair you add to the hook shank; however, after each clump is added, press each clump to the back of the hook shank by using your fingernails as shown in the illustration.

Note: The tighter you press the clumps of hair together, the better result you will have when you trim your fly.

WINGS

WING MATERIALS

Many types of materials can be used for wings, such as hair fibers, hackle tips, quill segments, and the like. For the most part, they are all applied to the hook in the same fashion. However, depending on the type of fly you are tying (dry, wet, or streamer) and the position of the wings, some variations in the application will be necessary.

The following illustrations show the basic steps required to attach the wings. The illustrations show quill segments used for the pattern in what is called a down-wing position.

BASIC WING ATTACHMENT

STEP 1

Position the material in its proper location, holding it tightly and grasping the hook at the same time with the same fingers, and give it two loose wraps with the thread.

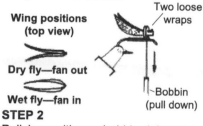

Wing positions (top view)

Dry fly—fan out

Wet fly—fan in

Two loose wraps

Bobbin (pull down)

STEP 2

Pull down with your bobbin, tightening the two wraps. Add an additional wrap behind the material and three more at the front.

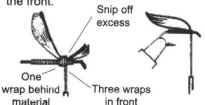

Snip off excess

One wrap behind material

Three wraps in front

UPRIGHT WINGS

The following illustrations show how to tie in the wings in the upright position using quill segments or hair fibers for most dry fly patterns.

QUILL OR HACKLE WINGS

Upright wings are tied in the same way as the basic wing attachment, except that the butt end of the material is held at the front of the hook, rather than the back end. In addition, after the loose wraps are tightened, the wing is pulled upright and a few wraps are made at the front and back of the material to keep it in the upright position.

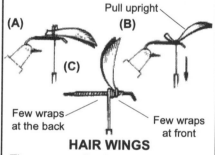

Pull upright

(A)　　(B)

(C)

Few wraps at the back

Few wraps at front

HAIR WINGS

The same application described above applies for hair wing patterns. If you want to separate the hairs into two wings, apply the following procedure.

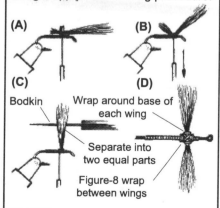

(A)　　(B)

(C)　　(D)

Bodkin

Wrap around base of each wing

Separate into two equal parts

Figure-8 wrap between wings

WATERFOWL FEATHERS

For the most part, game cock feathers are the most frequently used feathers in fly tying. Nevertheless, waterfowl such as ducks and geese also provide important feathers used in the construction of most patterns. The following illustrations show the feathers that are used, their names, descriptions, and locations on the bird, and their applications on various types of patterns.

PRIMARIES or POINTERS:

The first six long pointer feathers found on the wing tip of both geese and ducks, which have very heavy quills. Segments from these feathers are used to make wings on most dry or wet fly patterns and are also used for wing cases for nymph patterns. The biots found on the leading edge of the first wing feather from a goose are also used for tails on nymph patterns.

SECONDARIES or FLIGHTS:

The ten shorter feathers found on the wing nearer the bird's body. These heavy quilled, blunt feathers are used for making wings on dry or wet fly patterns.

BREAST:

Feathers found on ducks at the lower throat, covering the breast area of the bird. The feathers are stiff quilled, short, wide, and curved and have barred markings. They are used for dry and wet fly wings, and tails and shoulders for streamer patterns.

FLANK:

Found along the sides of ducks, the feathers are pointed and wide with distinctive markings. Used for dry fly wings, streamer shoulders and tailing.

FEATHER NAMES AND LOCATIONS

Primaries or pointers

Secondaries or flights

Flank feathers

Breast feathers

TYPICAL WATERFOWL (Duck)

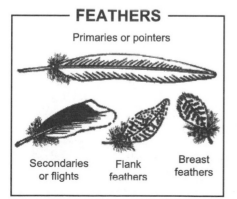

FEATHERS

Primaries or pointers

Secondaries or flights

Flank feathers

Breast feathers

HACKLES

When a pattern calls for a hackle to be used for a collar, beard or palmered body, the proper type of hackle selection can be important. Shown below are a few characteristics to consider when selecting the hackle for your fly.

1. Hackles used for dry flies are selected by the length of the barbules (which should be one and a half times the gap of the hook) and by the lack of webbing in the feather. Most dry fly hackles come from a rooster or male bird.

2. Hackles for wet flies and streamers should be the softer, webby-type feathers. These feathers will absorb water readily. They come for the most part from a hen or female bird.

3. Most dry flies use saddle or neck hackles, while in wet fly patterns the spade or spey hackles are used.

4. Hackles to be used for collars (spun) should have as little webbing as possible.

5. Hackles used for beards or palmering can either be a wet or dry fly type of feather.

HACKLE PREPARATION

Either of the following ways of preparing a hackle should be done before tying it onto the hook.

Strip off soft fluffy material at the bottom of the feather

Trim off soft fluffy material at the bottom of the feather with your scissors, leaving stubble-like barbs.

PALMERED HACKLES

When a hackle is tied in at one point **(A)** on the hook shank and is then wound **(B)** along its length and tied off at another point **(C)**, the hackle is called a palmered hackle. This technique is called palmering and is used in a variety of patterns.

Starting point

Finishing point

(A)   **(B)**   **(C)**

HACKLING TECHNIQUES

HACKLE COLLAR

SPINNING: When a hackle is wound in at the same location on the hook shank, it is called a spun hackle. Most spun hackles are used on dry flies or streamers when the pattern calls for a hackle collar. The hackle can be tied in by the tip end **(A)** or by the butt end **(B),** and then spun around the hook shank as shown below **(C, D).**

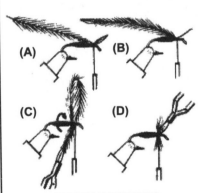

(A)   **(B)**

(C)   **(D)**

HACKLE BEARDS

Beards can be tied in using various techniques.
(A) They can be a spun hackle pulled down and tied into position with some additional wraps of your thread.
(B) They can be loose hackle barbules tied in under the hook shank.
(C) They can be a hackle tip cut into a "V" notch and then tied in and pulled into position.

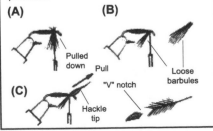

(A)   **(B)**

Pulled down   Pull   Loose barbules

(C)   "V" notch   Hackle tip

FLY PATTERN PARTS

The various parts of a fly that may be incorporated into a fly pattern are shown below. The materials to be used for each part may vary depending on the type of pattern (dry fly, wet fly, streamer). Not all patterns will include all the parts shown.

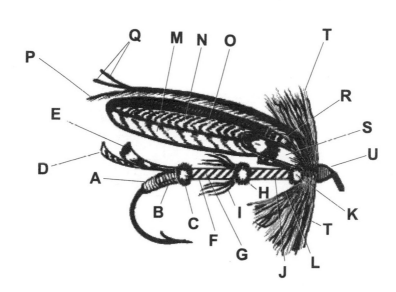

A. Tag: tinsel
B. Tip: floss
C. Butt: peacock herl or ostrich herl
D. Tail: feather segment
E. Tail topping: feather segment
F. Ribbing: tinsel
G. Body: floss or wool
H. Center joint: peacock herl or ostrich herl
I. Trailers: feather barbules
J. Forward body: floss or wool
K. Forward joint: peacock herl or ostrich herl
L. Beard: feather barbules

M. Underwing: feather, feather segment or buck tail
N. Upperwing: feather, feather segment or buck tail
O. Overwing: feather, feather segment or buck tail
P. Topping: golden pheasant crest feather
Q. Horns: single feather fibers
R. Shoulder: feather, feather segment
S. Cheek: feather
T. Collar: spun hackle feather
U. Head: thread

FLY PATTERN PROPORTIONS

The following illustrations show the standard proportions to use when constructing dry and wet fly patterns.

——— DRY FLY PROPORTIONS ———

TAIL: 1-1/2 times the body
BODY: Shank length less head
WING: Height equals shank length; width equals gap width
HACKLE: Equals 1-1/2 times the gap
HEAD: Equals eye width

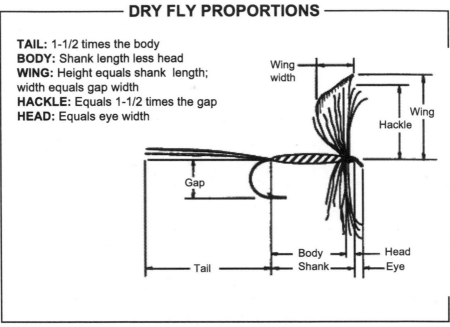

——— WET FLY PROPORTIONS ———

TAIL: Equals body length
BODY: Shank length less head
WING: Length equals hook length; width equals gap width
BEARD: Equals body length
HEAD: Equals eye width

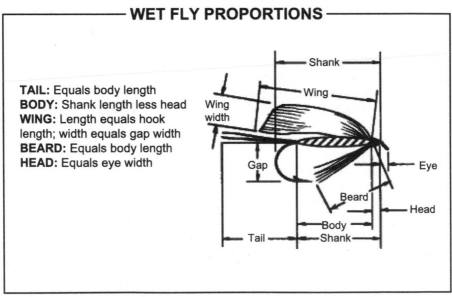

FLY PATTERN PROPORTIONS

The following illustrations show the standard proportions to use when constructing streamer and nymph fly patterns.

STREAMER FLY PROPORTIONS

TAIL: 1/2 of the body
BODY: Shank length less head
WING: Length equals tail plus body length

BEARD: Equals width of hook gap
HEAD: 1/8" to 3/16"

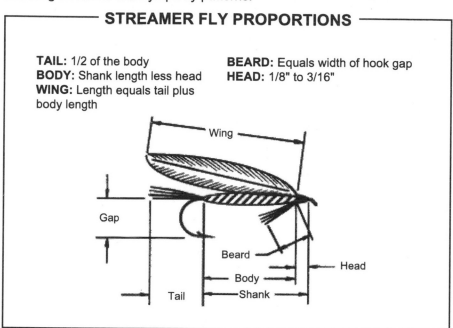

NYMPH FLY PROPORTIONS

TAIL: Equals body length
BODY: Shank length less head (includes thorax and abdomen)
ABDOMEN: 1/2 body length
THORAX: 1/2 body length
WING CASE: 1/2 body length
LEGS: Equal to body length
HEAD: 1/16" to 1/8"

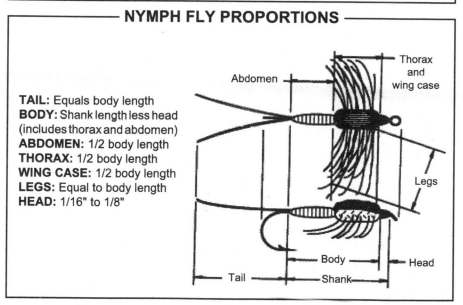

HOW TO TIE A DRY FLY

The illustrations on this page and the next show the basic steps used to tie an Adams, a dry fly pattern that is a simple but very effective trout pattern and the most popular dry fly in the country.

REQUIRED MATERIALS
HOOK: Mustad #94840
SIZE: #10 through #18
THREAD: Black 6/0
TAIL: Brown and grizzly hackle fibers (mixed)
BODY: Gray muskrat dubbing
WING: Two grizzly hackle tips
HACKLE: One brown and one grizzly hackle

STEP 3
Pull the hackle tips into an upright position, add a few wraps in front of them and divide them with a figure-8 knot. Then bring your thread behind the wings.

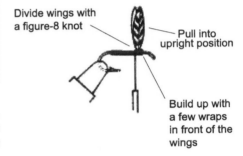

Divide wings with a figure-8 knot

Pull into upright position

Build up with a few wraps in front of the wings

STEP 1
Form a thread base on the hook shank, leaving a short section of the shank bare behind the hook eye equal to the eye of the hook.

Bare area equal to the hook eye

STEP 2
Select two grizzly saddle hackles for the wings and strip off the barbules until the tips are the length of the hook shank. Tie in the hackle tips as shown below at a point on the shank that is equal to twice the size of the hook eye.

STEP 4
Select brown and grizzly hackles that have fibers one and a half times as long as the gap of the hook. Strip back the fluff at the base of each feather and tie them in behind the wing, as shown below.

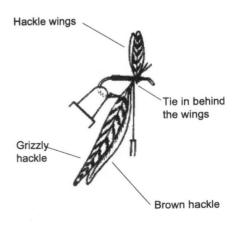

Hackle wings

Tie in behind the wings

Grizzly hackle

Brown hackle

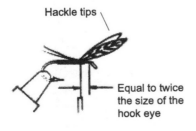

Hackle tips

Equal to twice the size of the hook eye

Fly Tying

STEP 5
Bring your thread back to the bend of the hook. Select a small bunch of hackle fibers (barbules) from a brown and grizzly hackle and mix them up. Then even up the tips with your hair stacker or by hand, and tie them in at the bend of the hook. The hackle fibers (barbules) should be one and a half times the length of the body.

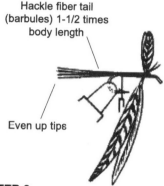

Hackle fiber tail (barbules) 1-1/2 times body length

Even up tips

STEP 6
After the tail is in place, bring your thread mid-way between the tail and the wing. Add dubbing to the thread and start forming the body by wrapping back on the shank to the bend and then going forward to the wing. Build up the body so that it is tapered and thicker toward the wing. After the body is complete, bring your thread forward in front of the wing.

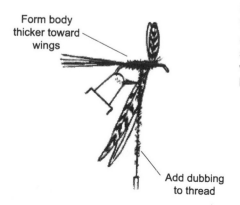

Form body thicker toward wings

Add dubbing to thread

STEP 7
Grasp one of the hackle tips that was tied in earlier with a pair of hackle pliers, and give it two wraps behind the wing and two wraps in front of the wing. Secure it with your thread and snip off the excess.

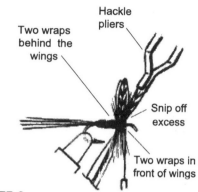

Hackle pliers

Two wraps behind the wings

Snip off excess

Two wraps in front of wings

STEP 8
Repeat the wrapping process as in step 7 with the second hackle, secure it with your thread, and snip off the excess.

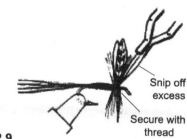

Snip off excess

Secure with thread

STEP 9
With your free hand, pull back the hackles at the front of the wing and form a neat, small head with your thread. Tie off with a whip finish and give the head a coat of head cement.

HOW TO TIE A WET FLY

The following illustrations show the basic steps used to tie a Royal Coachman (wet style), which is a very effective pattern dating back to the 1830s.

REQUIRED MATERIALS

HOOK: Mustad #3906 or #3906B
SIZE: #10 through #16
THREAD: Black 6/0
TAIL: Golden pheasant tippet fibers
BODY: Peacock herl and red floss
HACKLE: Brown
WING: White duck quill sections from a matched pair of quills

---

STEP 1

Starting with the matched duck quills, cut out the wing segments, as shown below, by using the gap of the hook to get the proper width for each wing. After the wing segments are cut, put them aside until later and secure the hook in your vise.

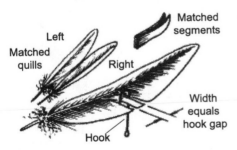

Matched quills
Left
Matched segments
Right
Width equals hook gap
Hook

STEP 2

Form a thread base on the hook shank, leaving a short section of the shank bare behind the hook eye equal to the width of the eye.

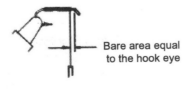

Bare area equal to the hook eye

STEP 3

Select a small bunch of fibers (three or four) from a golden pheasant tippet feather and tie them in as the tail at the bend of the hook. The fibers that extend beyond the bend should be equal to the body length. *NOTE: When you tie in the tail, wrap it in over the entire body area to prevent bumps when the body is tied in.*

Golden pheasant tippets equal to body length
Snip off excess
Wrap over entire body area

STEP 4

Tie in a couple of peacock herls and a 12" piece of red floss over the entire body area and back to the point where the tail was tied in at the hook bend. Then make about six wraps over the material, bringing your thread forward.

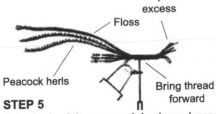

Snip off excess
Floss
Peacock herls
Bring thread forward

STEP 5

Take both of the peacock herls and wrap them over each other to form a ball (butt) at the bend of the hook. Secure them with your thread, and then bring your thread forward, wrapping over the remaining herl to within 3/16" of the eye.

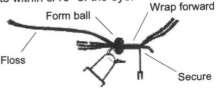

Wrap forward
Form ball
Floss
Secure

Fly Tying

STEP 6

Take the red floss and wrap forward, forming the body, up to the point where you stopped with your thread. Secure the floss with a few wraps and snip off the excess.

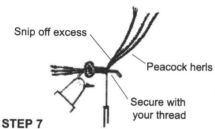

Snip off excess

Peacock herls

Secure with your thread

STEP 7

With the remaining peacock herl form another butt in front of the floss body as you did in step 5. Secure the herl with your thread and snip off what's left.

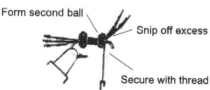

Form second ball

Snip off excess

Secure with thread

STEP 8

Take the brown hackle feather and strip off the barbule on one side and the fluff at the bottom on the opposite side. Tie in the hackle by the tip end (A) in front of the second ball and give it two to three wraps around the shank. Secure it with your thread and cut away the remaining hackle (B).

(A)   **(B)**

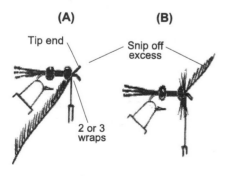

Tip end

Snip off excess

2 or 3 wraps

STEP 9

(A) Take the wing segments that you made earlier and match them up, with the tips pointing inward as shown below. (B) Grasp both wing segments with your free hand and place them in front of the hackle over the spot where thay are to be tied in. *NOTE: Be sure that the tips are in the downward position toward the hook shank.* (C) Put two loose wraps over the wings and pull down with your bobbin while holding the wings as tightly as possible, and then make a few more wraps with your thread before releasing the wings. (D) After the wings are in place, snip off the excess material and form a neat head with your thread.

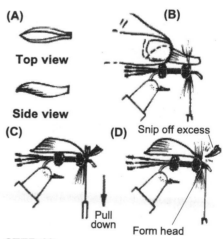

(A)   **(B)**

Top view

Side view

(C)   **(D)** Snip off excess

Pull down   Form head

STEP 10

After the head is formed, tie off with a whip finish and coat the head with cement. Your Royal Coachman is now complete.

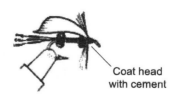

Coat head with cement

HOW TO TIE A STREAMER FLY

The following illustrations show the basic steps used to tie a Black Ghost, which is a simple but very effective streamer fly pattern.

REQUIRED MATERIALS

HOOK: Mustad #9575 or #79580
SIZE: #2 through #12
THREAD: Black 6/0
TAIL: Yellow hackle barbules
BODY: Black floss or wool
RIBBING: Flat silver tinsel
WING: Four white saddle hackles
BEARD: Yellow hackle barbules
CHEEK: Jungle cock

STEP 1
Form a thread base on the hook shank, leaving a short section of the shank bare behind the hook eye (about 1/8" to 3/16"), and bring the thread back to the hook bend.

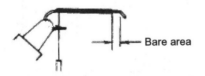

Bare area

STEP 2
Remove some barbules from a yellow saddle hackle and tie them in just in front of the bend of the hook. The barbules should be about half the body length.

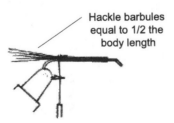

Hackle barbules equal to 1/2 the body length

STEP 3
Attach the black floss or wool for the body and the silver tinsel ribbing at the point where the tail was tied in. Then bring your thread forward to the front of the hook.

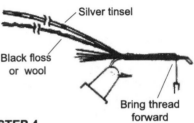

Silver tinsel

Black floss or wool

Bring thread forward

STEP 4
Using the black floss or wool, wrap the shank, forming a tapered body as shown below. After the body is formed, secure it with your thread and snip off the excess material.

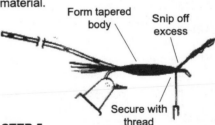

Form tapered body

Snip off excess

Secure with thread

STEP 5
Next, take the flat silver tinsel ribbing and wrap it over the body in neat even spirals. Secure the tinsel with your thread and snip off the excess.

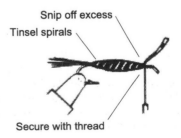

Snip off excess

Tinsel spirals

Secure with thread

STEP 6

Next, add the beard. Take another small bunch of yellow hackle barbules and tie them in at the front of the body under the hook shank as shown. The hackle barbules should be the width of the hook gap. Snip off the excess material and secure the beard with a few additional wraps of your thread.

STEP 7

After the beard is in place, select four white saddle hackles that will be equal to the body length plus the tail after the fluff is removed from the base of each feather. Remove the fluff and pair up the feathers. Take the two pairs and match up the tips, with the concave side of each pair facing in. Then grasp all four feathers at the base and position them over the tie-in point, and make two loose wraps (A). Pull down with your bobbin while holding the feathers, and tighten up on the thread (B). Make an additional few wraps before releasing the feathers. Snip off the excess materials and again add a few more wraps.

STEP 8

Take the jungle cock cheeks and remove the fluff at the base of each feather. Tie in the cheeks one at a time, making sure that they are in the same location and position on each side of the fly. The length of each cheek should be no longer than half the body length. Snip off the remaining hackle stems.

STEP 9

After the cheeks are in place, build up a neat tapered head with your thread and tie off with a whip finish. Coat the head with cement and allow it to dry. Your Black Ghost streamer is now complete.

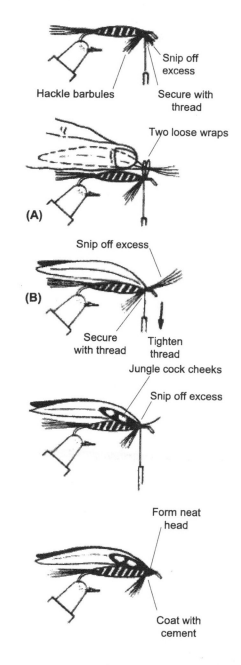

Hackle barbules — Snip off excess — Secure with thread

Two loose wraps

(A)

Snip off excess

(B) Secure with thread — Tighten thread

Jungle cock cheeks — Snip off excess

Form neat head

Coat with cement

HOW TO TIE A NYMPH FLY

The following illustrations show the basic steps used to tie a nymph fly. The pattern selected is a general type of black nymph that includes most of the steps involved when tying a nymph pattern.

REQUIRED MATERIALS
HOOK: Mustad #38941 or #9671
SIZE: #8 through #14
THREAD: Black 6/0
TAIL: Black goose quill biots
BODY: Weighted with fuse wire or solder and tied in two equal parts
ABDOMEN: Black dubbing (ribbed)
THORAX: Black dubbing (palmered)
RIBBING: Thin copper wire
LEGS: Black hackle feather (palmered)
WING CASE: Black goose quill segment
HEAD: Black Thread

STEP 1
Form a thread base on the hook shank, leaving a short section of the shank bare behind the hook eye (about 1/16" to 1/8").

Bare area

STEP 2
Take a 3" to 4" piece of fuse wire or solder and wrap it around the center two thirds of the hook shank. Snip off the excess and secure it with your thread by winding through the wire and putting a few wraps at the front and back. Bring your thread to the bend of the hook.

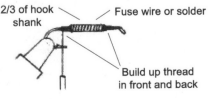

2/3 of hook shank — Fuse wire or solder

Build up thread in front and back

STEP 3
Build a small ball of thread at the bend and, behind the ball, tie in a pair of goose biots as the tail. Tie the biots in at an angle, as shown below.

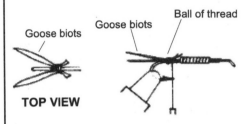

Ball of thread

Goose biots

Goose biots

TOP VIEW

STEP 4
Tie in the copper wire ribbing under the hook shank at the point where the tail was tied in.

Copper wire

STEP 5
Using a sparse amount of black dubbing, dub the thread and wrap about half of the area between the tail and the tie-in point for the abdomen. Build up the forward end of the dubbed area to a slight taper, as shown below.

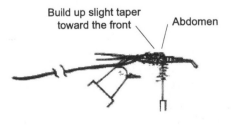

Build up slight taper toward the front

Abdomen

Fly Tying

STEP 6

After you finish building the abdomen, wrap the copper wire ribbing around the dubbed abdomen in neat even spirals, as shown below. Secure it with your thread and snip off the excess.

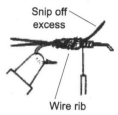

Snip off excess

Wire rib

STEP 7

Cut out a 1/8" to 3/16" wide segment from a black goose quill for the wing case. Coat the segment with a light application of head cement and allow it to dry. After it dries, tie it in at the front of the abdomen on top of the hook shank, with the dull side up.

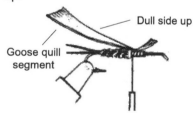

Dull side up

Goose quill segment

STEP 8

At the same point, tie in the black saddle hackle (by the feather tip) which will be used for the legs.

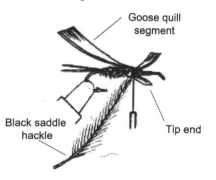

Goose quill segment

Black saddle hackle

Tip end

STEP 9

Add more black dubbing to your thread and wrap the thorax portion of the body. This area should be thicker than the abdomen, as shown below.

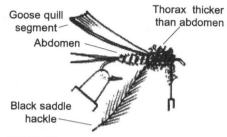

Goose quill segment

Thorax thicker than abdomen

Abdomen

Black saddle hackle

STEP 10

After you finish dubbing the thorax, palmer the black saddle hackle over the thorax, and secure it with your thread.

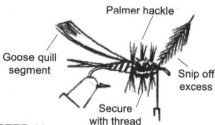

Palmer hackle

Goose quill segment

Snip off excess

Secure with thread

STEP 11

Bring the wing case (goose quill segment) over the top of the thorax, secure it with your thread, and cut off the excess.

Snip off excess

STEP 12

Build a neat head with your thread, tie off with a whip finish, and give the head a coat of cement. Your black nymph is now complete.

Coat with cement

ASSORTED PATTERNS

BEARTRACKS BI-VISIBLE

Nymph—Trout

HOOK: Mustad #94840 or #94845
SIZE: #14 to #22
THREAD: Brown
TAG: Flat gold tinsel
TAIL: Brown hackle fibers
BODY: Rear third generous ball of peacock herl, middle third brown hackle fibers equal to the hook gap, front third cream hackle fibers twice as wide as the gap
HEAD: Brown thread

BLUE ZULU

Wet—Trout

HOOK: Mustad #3906B
SIZE: #8 to #14
THREAD: Black
TAIL: Short section of red wool
BODY: Black wool, seal, or ostrich herl
RIB: Fine flat silver tinsel followed by a palmered black hackle
HACKLE: Three turns of a long-fibered blue hackle tied in front of the body
HEAD: Bright red thread

BOSS

Hairwing—Steelhead

HOOK: Mustad #7970
SIZE: #4 to #6
THREAD: Black 3/0
TAIL: Black squirrel, twice the length of the hook
BODY: Black chenille
RIB: Medium oval silver tinsel
HACKLE: Red or orange (collared)
EYES: Bead chain

Fly Tying

CHIEF NEEDABEH

Streamer—Trout

HOOK: Mustad #9575
SIZE: #6 to #8
THREAD: Black
TAG: Flat silver tinsel
BODY: Scarlet floss
RIB: Oval silver tinsel
WING: Two yellow hackles (back-to-back) with two orange hackles outside
HACKLE: Yellow hackle with red hackle in front, both wound and collared
CHEEKS: Jungle cock or substitute
HEAD: Black thread

DUCKY DARLING

Streamer—Trout

HOOK: Mustad #90240
SIZE: #4 to #10
THREAD: Black 6/0
WING: Woodchuck guard hair fibers
TAIL: Woodchuck guard hair fibers
BODY: Blend of fawn tan and rusty orange dubbing fur
HACKLE: Grizzly and brown mixed

FILOPLUME MAYFLY

Nymph—Trout

HOOK: Tiemco #200
SIZE: #12 to #20
THREAD: Body color
TAIL: Marabou—body color
RIB: Copper wire
BODY: Marabou—olive, brown, black or gray
WING CASE: Peacock sword fibers
THORAX: Filoplume—body color
HEAD: Thread—body color

FINCH
Nymph—Trout

HOOK: Mustad #3906B
SIZE: #14 to #16
THREAD: Black
ABDOMEN: Fur dubbing, antron or crystal flash
THORAX: Peacock herl
COLLAR: Partridge or hen saddle hackle
LEGS: Partridge hackle
HEAD: Black thread

GREEN BUTT SKUNK
Hairwing—Steelhead

HOOK: Mustad #36890
SIZE: #1 to #6
THREAD: Black
TAIL: Red hackle fibers
BUTT: Two to three turns of fluorescent green chenille
BODY: Black chenille
RIB: Flat silver tinsel
HACKLE: Black
WING: White buck tail or calf tail

LADY GODIVA
Hairwing—Steelhead

HOOK: Eagle Claw #1197B
SIZE: #1/0 to #6
THREAD: Black
TIP: Flat silver tinsel
TAIL: Mixed yellow and red hackle fibers
BUTT: Red chenille
BODY: White yarn
RIB: Flat silver tinsel
WING: Bright red polar bear
HEAD: Black thread

Fly Tying

LIGHT CAHILL
Dry—Trout

HOOK: Mustad #94840
SIZE: #10 to #20
THREAD: Cream or pale yellow
WING: Lemon yellow wood duck flank feather fibers
TAIL: Dark cream hackle fibers
BODY: Creamy yellow fur dubbing
HACKLE: Dark cream

MONTANA NYMPH
Nymph—Trout

HOOK: Mustad #9672 or #38941
SIZE: #2 to #12
THREAD: Black
TAIL: Few strands of short black crow feather
BODY: Black chenille
THORAX: Yellow chenille, ribbed with a moderately long, soft black hackle
WING CASE: Two strands of black chenille tied down over the top of the thorax
HEAD: Black thread

PALE EVENING DUN
Dry—Trout

HOOK: Mustad #94840
SIZE: #14 to #20
THREAD: Cream or primrose 6/0
WING: Light dun hackle tips
TAIL: Light blue dun hackle fibers
BODY: Pale yellow fur dubbing
HACKLE: Light blue dun

PARMACHENE BELLE
Wet—Trout

HOOK: Mustad #3906
SIZE: #8 to #14
THREAD: Black
TAIL: Mixed red and white hackle barbules
BODY: Yellow floss
RIB: Flat gold tinsel
WING: Married section of red and white duck wing quill segments (red on top)
HACKLE: Mixed red and white hackles
HEAD: Black thread

PRINCE NYMPH
Nymph—Trout

HOOK: Mustad #7957BX
SIZE: #6 to #10
THREAD: Black silk
TAIL: Goose biots (cocoa brown) tied in on either side of the hook and flared with the thumbnail
BODY: Peacock herl twisted counter-clockwise
RIB: Gold tinsel
HACKLE: Sparse brown hackle, collared and clipped on top
WINGS: Two white goose biots crossed at 30° and tightly wound with thread

RENEGADE
Wet—Steelhead

HOOK: Mustad #3135 or #34007
SIZE: #4 to #6
THREAD: Black
TAIL: Red calf tail or polar bear
REAR HACKLE: Soft dark brown saddle hackle
RIB: Variegated metallic thread
BODY: Prime peacock herl (ribbed)
FRONT HACKLE: Soft white saddle hackle
HEAD: Black thread

SPITFIRE
Wet—Trout

HOOK: Mustad #3906B
SIZE: #8 to #14
THREAD: Black 6/0
TAIL: Slip of red duck quill
RIB: Brown hackle (folded)
BODY: Black chenille
HACKLE: Guinea hen (collared)
WING: None

SKINNER'S CENTENNIAL
Streamer—Trout

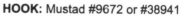

HOOK: Mustad #9672 or #38941
SIZE: #2 to #10
THREAD: Black
TAIL: Scarlet red hackle fibers
BODY: Black dubbing or wool
RIB: Flat silver tinsel
WING: Two scarlet red hackles flanked by two black saddle hackles
CHEEKS: Jungle cock
COLLAR: Black hackle collared and tied back
HEAD: Black thread

THE THIEF
Muddler—Crappie

HOOK: Mustad #9672
SIZE: #2 to #12
THREAD: Black
TAIL: Small red section of duck wing feather as long as the gap of the hook and tied upright
BODY: Wound silver tinsel
WING: A bunch of gray squirrel tail extending slightly beyond the tail with a fairly wide section of turkey wing feather on each side as long as the squirrel tail hairs
HEAD: Several turns of black chenille

UMPQUA SPECIAL
Buck tail—Trout

HOOK: Mustad #36890
SIZE: #1/0 to #8
THREAD: Black
TAIL: White buck tail
BODY: Rear third yellow wool, front two thirds red wool or chenille
RIB: Narrow oval silver tinsel from tail to head
WING: Sparse white buck tail extending just beyond the tail
SHOULDERS: Narrow strip of red goose feather or buck tail
THROAT: Dark brown hackle, collared

WEENEY MACSWEENEY
Wet—Trout

HOOK: Mustad #3906B
SIZE: #10
THREAD: Black
TAG: Silver wire
BODY: Two thirds black floss, ribbed with silver wire; front third fluorescent magenta floss
WING: Black squirrel tail (sparse)
HACKLE: Scarlet cock feather (long fiber) tied full and collared
HEAD: Black thread

WOODCHUCK WULFF
Dry—Trout

HOOK: Mustad #90240
SIZE: #4 to #10
THREAD: Black 6/0
WING: Woodchuck guard hair fibers
TAIL: Woodchuck guard hair fibers
BODY: Blend of fawn tan and rusty orange dubbing fur
HACKLE: Grizzly and brown mixed